POLYMORPHISM IN JAVA

POLYMORPHISM IN JAVA

Methods and polymorphic algorithms applied to computer games

First edition 2018

Author: Carlos Alberto Privitera

Advanced level

Book information:
- Title: Polymorphism in Java
- Edition: 1st edition 2018
- Author: Carlos Alberto Privitera
- ISBN-13: 978-1725953420
- ISBN-10: 1725953420
- Date of the first edition: spring 2018

About the Author:

Carlos Alberto Privitera is a specialist in Java SE and has been dedicated to the construction of computer systems with Java SE since 2000. He has extensive experience in teaching the Java language. He has specialized in creating content to teach courses on the Java SE language.
It has the titles of:
- "Técnico Analista de Sistemas de información" awarded by the "Instituto Superior de Informática 9-012".
- "Licenciado en Educación" awarded by the "Universidad Nacional de Quilmes".
- "Profesor en Ciencias de la Computación" awarded by the "Universidad de Mendoza".
- "Magister en Ingeniería del Software" awarded by the "Instituto Técnico de Buenos Aires".

Additional material on the Web
- https://libropolimorfismoenjava.blogspot.com/
- https://github.com/carlosprivitera

Contact with the author of the book:
- carlosprivitera@yahoo.com.ar

Dedication:

To my children

Foreword

This book stands out for teaching programming based on polymorphism. Abundant examples in Java code and illustrative graphics of the main ideas related to the topic: Polymorphism in Java.

The book "Polymorphism in Java" aims to give a modern and updated vision when learning Java and in the particular subject of polymorphic algorithms. Students, teachers and developers will be able to find a sequence of design patterns that create and use polymorphic algorithms, these design patterns can be applied to solving problems of computer systems and everyday life.

A professional in the Java language can benefit from the book "Polymorphism in Java" by finding an innovative way to solve problems with polymorphic algorithms. The design patterns, analyzed in this work, are based on the inheritance between classes. Currently the difficulties of the Java language have been overcome to a large extent and it is easy to understand and apply.

The book aims to teach fundamental concepts of object-oriented programming with Java SE, in a clear and practical way, significantly reducing the learning curve. In the process you will learn to program computers and use the Java SE language.

Goals:

- The present work aims that readers get strong knowledge in computer programming with the Java SE language.
- Get the reader to acquire practical skills by using advanced Java SE concepts.
- Have the reader write computer programs based on object-oriented programming with the Java SE language.

Recipients of the book

The book is aimed at anyone who wants to learn to program computers with Java SE, also the book is very useful for people who want to teach the Java language. The professionals will find a modern and updated work worthy of being studied and put into practice. Level of the book: it is of advanced level. It requires knowledge of the basic details of the Java SE language.

Level of the book: it is of advanced level. It requires knowledge of the basic details of the Java SE language.

The content of the book is applicable to all operating systems.

How to continue after learning the content of this book?

The learning of computer programming with the Java SE language is the gateway to learning advanced content related to companies and corporate environments; it is advisable after learning the content of this book to start learning Java EE, Java Web or Java for cell phones, if the reader wishes.

Index of titles and subtitles

Content

Chapter I

Introduction

In the construction of a software product, different structures are defined that determine the architecture of the software that will be built. The basic structures in Java are the classes and the relationships between the classes. Many times, a structure forms a recurring pattern in the construction of a software product. A programmer attentive to identifying structures and patterns can define an appropriate architecture to solve problems or build software. A proper architecture is as important as the development process in software engineering.

A layer structure can determine an appropriate architecture to define specific functions that are placed as strata; each layer can be replaced by a new layer without affecting the others. A precise and unique communications interface must be defined between the layers.

Proposal for a basic architecture

Layer 1 - Application layer or view layer or software product
The layer of the software product is the layer that the user sees or should use, the application layer provide the functionalities that the user has requested or wants. The application layer is a concrete implementation of the design pattern. The application layer traditionally uses structured algorithms, but this time the polymorphic algorithms will be added.

Layer 2 - Use the pattern
Layer 2 must create objects of the pattern type, some are objects created at runtime and others are created at the design time of the application. Objects are considered artifacts that perform different functions; an artifact can invoke different behaviors to the design pattern. The different artifacts access a method interface. With access to the methods interface, polymorphic algorithms can be written that provide functions to the application layer.

Layer 3 - Polymorphism
Layer 3 is the layer where polymorphic methods and polymorphic algorithms are written. Layer 4 separates the implementation of the polymorphic algorithms from the implementation of the solution of the problem; the polymorphic algorithms express different ways of using a solution of a problem.

Layer 4 - Pattern structure
Layer 4 - Pattern structure: Layer 4 is the design pattern that implements the strategy that solves the problem that has been raised, the design pattern contains the specialized and traditional algorithms. Different patterns can be implemented depending on the problem to be solved. A pattern has the property of supporting the solution of many problems. A group of problems can be solved by a single pattern. A very simple and useful pattern is the pattern that has a generic superclass and many specialized subclasses in an algorithm. Java is a language that allows the creation of hierarchical class structures, classes are related through inheritance.

Design pattern based on inheritance

The following image shows a pattern of related classes through inheritance.

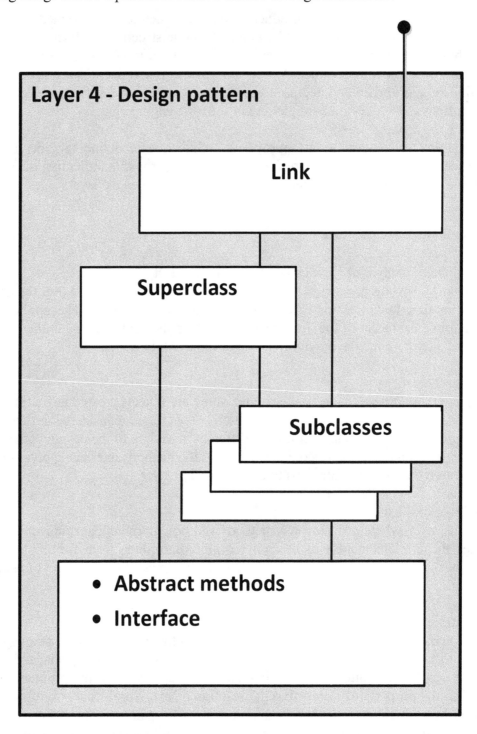

The image shows a generic representation of a design pattern based on the inheritance between classes. Certain restrictions will configure different design patterns more suitable to be implemented in Java.

Layered architecture to use a design pattern

The following image shows an architecture made by layers. Each layer has a certain function to implement, use and show the solution of a problem.

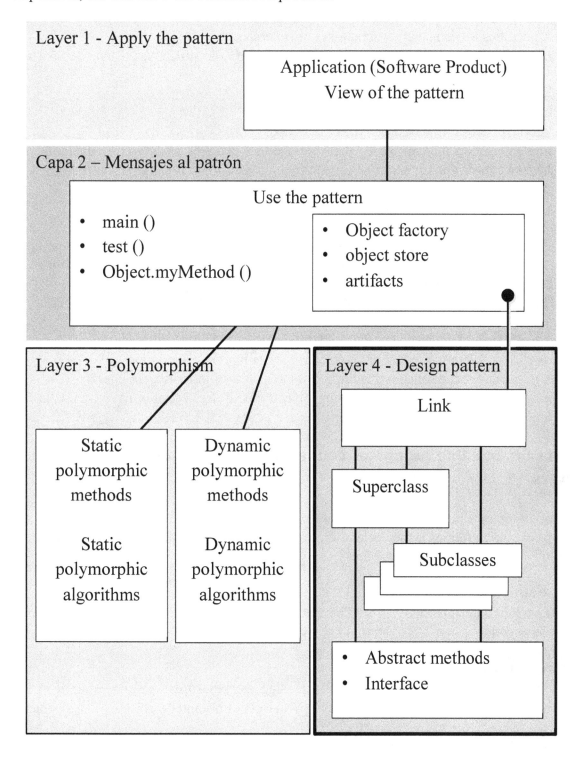

Description of the design pattern based on the inheritance

A design pattern based on inheritance has the following parts:
- A generic superclass
- Several specialized subclasses
- Algorithms implemented in subclasses or superclasses
- Inheritance relationship between the superclass and the subclasses using the Java keyword: `extends`
- Interface: public methods of access to private data
- Interface: of abstract methods
- Interface: declaration of prototypes of methods
- Implementation relationship of the interface that declares prototypes of methods using the Java keyword: `implements`
- Relationship of creation of objects between classes using the Java keyword: `new`

Types of relations between classes
1. The extension relationship joins two classes of the same type, one class extends another class.
2. The implementation relationship adds parts to a class; a class is added to another class to be implemented as a component part of the class.
3. The object creation relation indicates that a class has an object reference to an object instance.

Java has a keyword to declare each relationship
1. `extends`: relation of equal or extension types or inheritance relation
2. `implements`: relationship of adding parts to a class or inheriting an interface
3. `new`: relation of composing or using objects for a class, classes have or use instances of objects

Criteria for building groups of configurations of patterns of architectures by layers

The configurations can be divided into three groups, the criteria used to assemble the different groups of configurations is the declaration of abstract methods and the implementation of abstract methods by superclasses or subclasses.

What are abstract methods?
An abstract method has no body, { }. The method can not implement code since it has no body to write Java code.

What are abstract classes?
A class is abstract if it is declared as abstract using the keyword: `abstract`, or if at least one abstract method is declared in its body, { }. You can not instantiate objects of an abstract class.

What is an interface?
The interface is a totally abstract class; it does not have Java code in its body. The interface declares prototypes of abstract methods that will be inherited by other classes. Classes that inherit an interface should overwrite the abstract methods and implement the missing code.

There are two ways to declare abstract methods:
1. Declare methods using the keyword `abstract`
2. Declare prototypes of abstract methods in an interface

How to overwrite methods that are abstract?

There is a way to implement the missing code of abstract methods:
1. Overwrite abstract methods using the tag: `@Override`

Criteria for assembling the different configurations of a design pattern

The name of each configuration will depend on the creation of references to objects and the creation of objects.

What is a reference in Java?

This line of code is a statement of a reference to an object: `Rectangulo rectangulo = null;`

What is an object in Java?

This line of code is a declaration to create an instance of an object, given a reference: `rectangulo = new Rectangulo(3, 4);`

Programmers usually link the declaration of the reference and the creation of the object in a line of code. The following line of code is a declaration of a reference to an object and the creation of an object instance: `Rectangulo rectangulo = new Rectangulo(3, 4);`

Structure of the book

Graphical representation of the groups of configurations of a design pattern

Design pattern		
abstract classes		Interface
Group 1	Group 2	Group 3
Configurations	Configurations	Configurations
Variants	Variants	Variants
Polymorphism	Polymorphism	Mutable polymorphism

Definition of restrictions to assemble a design pattern

The restrictions are based on the possibility or impossibility of declaring:
2. References to objects
3. Instances of objects.

Group properties

	Create references	Create objects
Superclass		
Subclass		
Interface		

Group number one of configurations

In group number one, there are configurations where the superclass is declared abstract, within this group there are two configurations. Configuration number one declares the object reference using the name of the superclass and the creation of the objects using the constructors of the subclasses. The second configuration creates the reference of objects and objects using the subclasses.

This group has the fundamental characteristic that it prevents to create an object using the constructor of the superclass. When declaring the superclass as abstract, it is not possible in Java to create an object of an abstract class. In this group all the objects that can be created must be created using the constructors of the subclasses.

Group properties

	Create references	Create objects
Superclass (abstract)	Yes	Not allowed
Subclass	Yes	Yes

In group one there are two very interesting configurations that form an adequate architecture to use the inheritance pattern between classes.

Each configuration of the group includes an additional restriction that forces to make a correct use of the design pattern.

Structure of the design pattern

The design pattern is based on a superclass and many subclasses and different combinations that implement the interface of the abstract methods.

The design pattern must declare an interface of public methods that can be invoked by the classes that want to access the pattern. The design pattern is a provider of behaviors.

The design pattern has to be encapsulated in a package and allow or restrict one of the following four functions, depending on the problem you wish to solve.

1. Declare references of the subclasses or the superclass
2. Declare objects of the subclasses or the superclass
3. Inherit subclasses or superclasses for extension reasons
4. Overwrite the public methods of the design pattern for implementation reasons

In this book we will make a detailed study of the first two functions: 1) declare references of the subclasses or the superclass, 2) declare objects of the subclasses or the superclass.

The possibilities of extension and changes in the design pattern will be left out of the study, in this book. A detailed study will be made on the use of the design pattern by other classes. The classes that will use the design pattern are called "clients."

Classes that are clients of the design pattern may implement polymorphic methods and algorithms.

Configuration 1.1 - Create the object reference using the super class and the creation of the objects using the subclasses.

Java code to create the configuration 1.1

Variant 1 - a reference and an object in memory

```
SuperClase objeto = null;  //crear una referencia única
objeto = new SubClase01(); //apuntar la referencia a un nuevo objeto
...
objeto = new SubClase02(); //apuntar la referencia a un nuevo objeto
...
objeto = new SubClase03(); //apuntar la referencia a un nuevo objeto
...
objeto = new SubClaseN(); //apuntar la referencia a un nuevo objeto
```

Variant 2 - many references and one object by reference

```
SuperClase objeto1 = null;  //crear una referencia única
objeto1 = new SubClase01(); //apuntar la referencia a un nuevo objeto
...
SuperClase objeto2 = null;  //crear una referencia única
objeto2 = new SubClase02(); //apuntar la referencia a un nuevo objeto
...
SuperClase objeto3 = null;  //crear una referencia única
objeto3 = new SubClase03(); //apuntar la referencia a un nuevo objeto
...
SuperClase objetoN = null;  //crear una referencia única
objetoN = new SubClaseN(); //apuntar la referencia a un nuevo objeto
```

In the configuration 1.1 a new restriction is added, in the new restriction it is not advisable to create references of the subclasses. In this configuration there are two restrictions: it is not feasible to create objects of the superclass and it is not recommended to create references of the subclasses.

Properties of configuration 1.1

	Create references	**Create objects**
Superclass (abstract)	Yes	Not allowed
Subclass	X (restriction)	Yes

Utility of configuration 1.1
It is a suitable configuration for when there is a large number of specialized objects, each object has the need to implement a particular or unique algorithm.

This configuration has two variants:
1. A reference and an object in memory (consumes little memory). The garbage collector has a lot of work collecting old instances of unreferenced objects.
2. Many references and one object for each reference (consumes more memory). The garbage collector has little work.

If there is a reference there may be a specialized object in memory. The only reference works like a pointer that goes through the objects one by one. To access a new object you have to destroy the current object and build a new object.

If you have an object reference that points dynamically to different objects, it can happen that the use of memory is reduced but the work of the garbage collector Java is very arduous; On the other hand, when many references to objects are created, the use of memory is more likely to increase and the work of the garbage collector decreases.

Dynamic assignment of new objects to a single reference causes objects not referenced in memory to be cleaned by the Java garbage collector.

If the problem to be solved needs to create references to the subclasses, it would be appropriate to use the 1.2 configuration or another configuration of another group.

The dynamic assignment of the reference to a new object allows the application of the dynamic polymorphism mechanism, using the unique reference, unique messages can be sent to different specialized objects.

To apply or use the mechanism of the dynamic polymorphism, it is necessary to send messages to the objects through the methods interface. Each object must implement the same methods interface.

The messages are sent to the methods implemented in the objects, if all the objects implement the same methods interface then it is feasible to send the same message to each object. Each object will implement a different algorithm and behave differently even if the message sent is the same.

The programmers, are very creative, write algorithms based on objects that send messages. Algorithms based on sending messages are called polymorphic algorithms. Do not confuse message-based polymorphic algorithms with specialized algorithms that are implemented in the objects that receive the messages. Polymorphic algorithms are programmed in clients that use the class inheritance pattern; the specialized algorithms are programmed in the subclasses or superclasses of the pattern.

- Polymorphic algorithms send messages, (clients)
- Specialized algorithms receive messages. (providers)

Objects that receive messages from another object implement behavioral algorithms and algorithms that send messages to another object are called polymorphic algorithms.

From the point of view of the classes we can say that there are classes, clients, that send messages and classes, servants or suppliers, that respond to messages. The client classes implement polymorphic algorithms and the supplying classes implement behavioral or specialized algorithms.

Java classes have three mechanisms to implement interfaces of data access methods or algorithms that they implement.
1. Inherit an interface: the Java keyword "`implements`" is used.
2. Declare abstract methods: the Java keyword "`abstract`" is used.
3. Declare public methods of access to private or encapsulated data.

Layered Application Organization

Scheme that shows the relationship between: the algorithms that are polymorphic and the algorithms that have a specialized behavior.

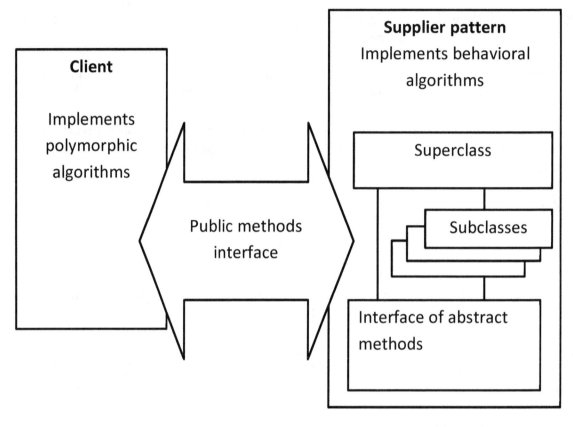

It is advisable to organize the system into at least two layers, one layer for classes that are clients and another layer for classes that are suppliers.

There are different ways to organize a Java application by layers:
1. A project with a package for all classes, (not recommended)
2. A project with two packages that will contain the classes assigned to each layer (recommended)
3. Two projects in one application, one project for each layer. (Recommended for teams of programmers or for large projects)

The same reasoning can be used if the application was designed with three or more layers. The packets may contain other packets so one layer may contain other layers or sublayers. In Java, a package is a folder created by the Operating System.

IDEs, (Integrated Development Environments), are tools that help create applications that will contain Java code projects. The projects will contain packages and the packages will contain files with source code written in the Java language.

Some popular IDEs to write Java code:
- JDeveloper: http://oracle.com
- NetBeans: https://netbeans.org/
- Eclipse: https://www.eclipse.org/
- IntelliJ: https://www.jetbrains.com/
- Visual Studio Code: https://code.visualstudio.com/
- Android Studio: https://developer.android.com/

Layer number one: client layer
- The package called "app" will contain the classes that are clients and the classes that implement the polymorphic algorithms.

Layer number two: provider layer
- The package called "patron" will contain the inheritance pattern between classes.

Java UML diagram for 1.1 configuration – Variant 1: A reference, an object in memory

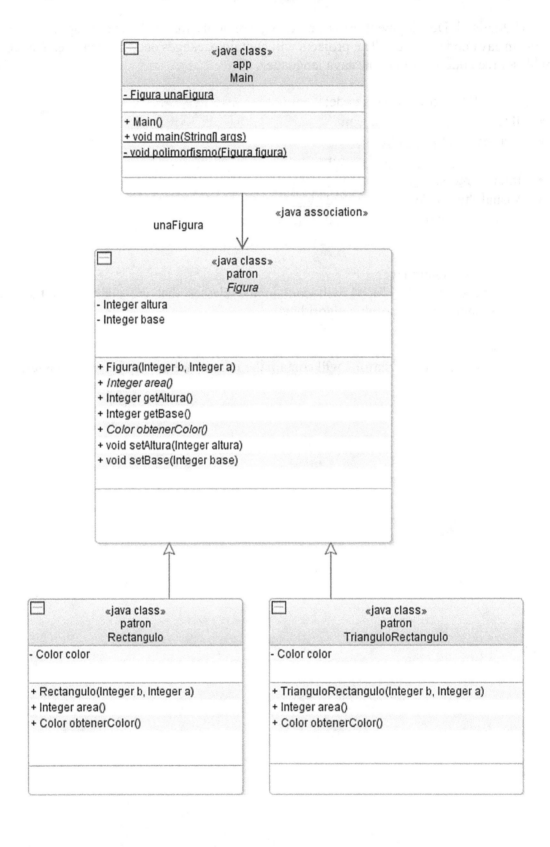

Source code for 1.1 Configuration – Variant 1

```
package app;

import patron.Figura;
import patron.Rectangulo;
import patron.TrianguloRectangulo;


public class Main {
    public Main() {
        super();
    }
    private static Figura unaFigura = null;

    public static void main(String[] args) {
        Main main = new Main(); //el objeto main tiene información relevante a
la clase Main{}

        //esto es un error, no es posible crear instancias de una clase
abstracta
        //Figura figura = new Figura();

        System.out.println("Polimorfismo dinámico o de referencia");

        unaFigura = new Rectangulo(6, 8);
        polimorfismo(unaFigura);

        unaFigura = new TrianguloRectangulo(6, 8);
        polimorfismo(unaFigura);

    } //Fin del cuerpo del método main()

    //Método polimórfico o sobrecargado por el argumento del parámetro
    //El parámetro acepta tipos de argumentos distintos
    //En algunas ocasiones el argumento es del tipo rectángulo
    //  y en otras es del tipo triángulo rectángulo

    private static void polimorfismo(Figura figura) {

        //Líneas polimórficas, tienen comportamiento distinto dependiendo de la
figura
        //El compilador Java decide que comportamiento ejecutar dependiendo del
tipo

        System.out.println(figura.getClass().getName());
        System.out.println("  Altura = " + figura.getAltura());
        System.out.println("  Base = " + figura.getBase());
        System.out.println("  Área " + figura.area());
        System.out.println("  Color " + figura.obtenerColor());

    } //Fin del cuerpo del método polimórfico
} //Fin del cuerpo de la clase Main{}
```

```java
package patron;

import java.awt.Color;

//Niveles de control de acceso public para clases, una clase pública puede ser
accedida por cualquier clase de cualquier paquete
//Una clase sin modificador puede ser accedida por una clase de su mismo paquete

public abstract class Figura {

    private Integer altura = 0;
    private Integer base = 0;

    public Figura(Integer b, Integer a) {
        base = b;
        altura = a;
        //super();
    }

    public void setAltura(Integer altura) {
        this.altura = altura;
    }

    public void setBase(Integer base) {
        this.base = base;
    }

    public Integer getAltura() {
        return altura;
    }

    public Integer getBase() {
        return base;
    }

    public abstract Integer area();

    public abstract Color obtenerColor();

}

package patron;

import java.awt.Color;

public class Rectangulo extends Figura {

    private Color color = new Color(0, 0, 0);

    public Rectangulo(Integer b, Integer a) {
        super(b, a); //Acceder a la estructura de datos de la superclase
        color = Color.orange;
    }

    @Override
    public Integer area() {
        return this.getAltura() * this.getBase();
    }
```

```
    @Override
    public Color obtenerColor() {
        // TODO Implement this method
        return color;
    }
}

package patron;

import java.awt.Color;

public class TrianguloRectangulo extends Figura {

    private Color color = new Color(0, 0, 0);

    public TrianguloRectangulo(Integer b, Integer a) {
        super(b, a); //Acceder a la estructura de datos de la superclase
        color = Color.green;
    }

    @Override
    public Integer area() {
        return (this.getAltura() * this.getBase()) / 2;
    }

    @Override
    public Color obtenerColor() {
        // TODO Implement this method
        return color;
    }

}
```

Explanation of the most relevant lines of code in the 1.1 Configuration – Variant 1

This line of code indicates that the class `Main{}` belongs to the package called `app`, the package called `app` will contain the classes of the layer named `client`.

```
package app;
```

Importing the classes from the package called `patron`. The package named `patron` will contain the classes of the layer named `proveedor`. Unfortunately, the 1.1 configuration must have access to all classes in the `proveedor` layer.

```
import patron.Figura;
import patron.Rectangulo;
import patron.TrianguloRectangulo;
```

Declaration of the `Main{}` class, the class named `Main{}` must be public. The JVM must find the `Main{}` class to create a memory instance.

```
public class Main {
```

Declaration of the constructor method called `Main()`, the `Main()` method must be public and homonymous to the `Main{}` class. The JVM will search and execute the `Main()` method at the time of creating an instance of the `Main{}` class.

Declaration of the constructor method, with the name of `Main()`. The `Main()` method must be public and homonym to the `Main{}` class. The JVM will search and execute the `Main()` method at the time of creating an instance of the `Main{}` class.

```
public Main() {
    super(); //invoca el constructor de la superclase Object
}
```

Declaration of the reference to objects with the name of: `unaFigura`. The `unaFigura` reference is of type `Figure{}`. The `unaFigura` reference is not pointing to an object instance.

```
private static Figura unaFigura = null;
```

Statement of the `main()` method, the `main()` method will be searched and executed by the JVM at the time of instantiating the `Main{}` class.

```
public static void main(String[] args) {

    Main main = new Main(); //el objeto main tiene información relevante a
la clase Main{}

    //esto es un error, no es posible crear instancias de una clase
abstracta
    //Figura figura = new Figura();

    System.out.println("Polimorfismo dinámico o de referencia, una
referencia muchos objetos, con recolector de basura");
```

This statement will point to the reference named `unaFigura` to the new object created by the constructor named `Rectangulo()`.

```
        unaFigura = new Rectangulo(6, 8);
```

The following line of code will execute the Polymorphic method called `polimorfismo()` with the parameter of type `Figura{}` and the argument of the type `Rectangulo{}`.

A method is polymorphic when the JVM must decide which method to execute depending on the type of parameter and the argument type. The JDK cannot predict at design time which method to run because it does not know the argument type of the parameter.

```
        polimorfismo(unaFigura);
```

The reference, called `unaFigura`, is pointed to a new object created by the constructor named `TrianguloRectangulo()`. The rectangle object does not have a valid reference and must be cleaned by the garbage collector. A reference is polymorphic if it is feasible to change the referenced object type.

```
    unaFigura = new TrianguloRectangulo(6, 8);
```

The following line of code executes the polymorphic method called `polimorfismo()`, the method has the parameter of type `Figura{}` and the argument of the parameter of type `TrianguloRectángulo{}`.

```
    polimorfismo(unaFigura);

} //Fin del cuerpo del método main()
```

The following code declares the dynamic polymorphic method called `polimorfismo()`, the dynamic polymorphic methods are characterized by having the parameters of a type and the arguments can be of another type. The parameter is of type `Figure{}` and the arguments can be of the type `Rectangulo{}` and `TrianguloRectangulo{}`. The dynamic polymorphic methods have polymorphic algorithms; the polymorphic algorithms are characterized by having different behaviors depending on the argument assigned to the parameter. Dynamic polymorphic methods send messages and are received by the classes that are providers of the different behaviors. The classes that are clients implement polymorphic algorithms and the classes that are providers implement specialized behavior algorithms. The main feature of dynamic polymorphic algorithms is that they change their behavior depending on the argument assigned to the parameter.

```
//Método polimórfico o sobrecargado por el argumento del parámetro
//El parámetro acepta tipos de argumentos distintos
//En algunas ocasiones el argumento es del tipo rectángulo
//  y en otras es del tipo triángulo rectángulo
private static void polimorfismo(Figura figura) {

    //Líneas polimórficas, tienen comportamiento distinto dependiendo de la
figura
    //El compilador Java decide que comportamiento ejecutar dependiendo del
tipo
    System.out.println(figura.getClass().getName());
    System.out.println("  Altura = " + figura.getAltura());
    System.out.println("  Base = " + figura.getBase());
    System.out.println("  Área " + figura.area());
    System.out.println("  Color " + figura.obtenerColor());


} //Fin del cuerpo del método polimórfico

}//Fin del cuerpo de la clase Main{}
```

Summary of Concepts:
- A method is polymorphic if it is overloaded in its parameters or arguments or both.
- An algorithm is polymorphic if it always sends the same message to classes that are providers of behaviors. The class, client, `Main{}` sends messages `getAltura()`, `getBase()`, `area()` y `getColor()` to classes that are providers of such behaviors.
- Classes that are customers implement polymorphic methods and algorithms, polymorphic methods, and polymorphic algorithms send messages to classes that are providers of specialized behaviors.

The classes that are providers implement a single method interface to receive messages from the classes that are clients.

This line of code indicates that the class named `Figura{}` belongs to the package named `patron`, the package with the `patron` name will contain the classes of the layer named `proveedor`.

```
package patron;
```

Statement to import the class named `Color` from the package named `java.awt`.

```
import java.awt.Color;
```

Class declaration with the name of `Figura{}`, the class named `Figura{}` must be public because it is invoked from the `app` package.

```
//Niveles de control de acceso de una clase
//1-Una clase pública puede ser accedida por cualquier clase de cualquier
  paquete
//2-una clase sin modificador puede ser accedida por una clase de su mismo
  paquete o desde otro paquete a través de la herencia

public abstract class Figura {
```

Declaration of the fields belonging to the class called `Figura{}`.

```
    private Integer altura = 0;
    private Integer base = 0;
```

Declaration of the constructor method called `Figura()`, the constructor method named `Figura()` must be public and homonymous to the class named `Figura{}`. The constructor is invoked at the time of creating an object instance. It is a good idea to use the constructor method to initialize the fields of the class. The constructor method is the primary interface for accessing private data in the class at the time of constructing an object. Constructor methods can be overloaded in their parameters and arguments.

```
    public Figura(Integer b, Integer a) {
        base = b;
        altura = a;
        //super();//No es necesario invocar el constructor de una superclase
    }
```

The following statements are the interface of public methods to access private data.

```
    public void setAltura(Integer altura) {
        this.altura = altura;
    }

    public void setBase(Integer base) {
        this.base = base;
    }

    public Integer getAltura() {
        return altura;
```

```
    }

    public Integer getBase() {
        return base;
    }
```

Declaration of the interface of abstract methods. Abstract methods must be overwritten, @Override, by the class that inherits this class.

```
    public abstract Integer area();

    public abstract Color obtenerColor();

}//Fin del cuerpo de la clase Figura{}
```

Summary of the main topics covered in the Java source code

Types of interfaces that can be declared in a class:
- Construction Methods
- Public methods
- Abstract Methods

Characteristics of a class declared as abstract:
- Cannot instantiate a class declared as abstract
- Class must be inherited to access non-static members
- If a class is declared abstract and not inherited, then it is preferable for all its public or protected members to be declared as static
- A class can be declared as abstract and not have abstract method statements. You cannot instantiate the class and force the class to be inherited, or that all its public or protected members are static
- If a class has an abstract method then the class must be declared abstract

In all method declarations, parameters and arguments can be overloaded.

In a method declaration, the overload of parameters and arguments is the mechanism that guarantees the construction of polymorphic algorithms.

This line of code indicates that the class named Rectangulo{} belongs to the package named patron, the package named patron will contain the classes of the layer named proveedor.

```
package patron;
```

```
import java.awt.Color;
```

Declaration of a class with the name Rectangulo{}. The class called Rectangulo{} must be public since it is invoked from the package called app. It also extends new functions and inherits the interface of public methods of access to private data declared in the inherited class.

```
public class Rectangulo extends Figura {
```

```
private Color color = new Color(0, 0, 0);
```

The methods that are constructors have access to the data structure of the inherited class; it is a good idea to initialize the data of the superclass when creating an instance of a subclass.

```
public Rectangulo(Integer b, Integer a) {
    super(b, a);//Ejecutar el constructor de la superclase. Acceder a
la estructura de datos de la superclase
    color = Color.orange;
}
```

The following lines of code overwrite, @Override, the legacy abstract methods. The methods that are declared abstract do not have code implemented; it is the subclass obligation to implement the missing code.

```
@Override
public Integer area() {
    return this.getAltura() * this.getBase();
}
```

```
@Override
public Color obtenerColor() {
    // TODO Implement this method
    return color;
}
```

```
}//Fin del cuerpo de la clase Rectangulo{}
```

It is not necessary to comment on the following code since it has been commented previously.

```
package patron;
```

```
import java.awt.Color;
```

```
public class TrianguloRectangulo extends Figura {
    private Color color = new Color(0, 0, 0);
    public TrianguloRectangulo(Integer b, Integer a) {
        super(b, a); //Acceder a la estructura de datos de la superclase
        color = Color.green;
    }
```

```
    @Override
    public Integer area() {
        return (this.getAltura() * this.getBase()) / 2;
    }
```

```
    @Override
    public Color obtenerColor() {
        // TODO Implement this method
        return color;
    }
```

```
}//Fin del cuerpo de la clase TrianguloRectangulo{}
```

Summary of the hierarchical structure of classes

The classes that are clients send messages to the subclasses; the subclasses manage the algorithms
implemented in their own body and the algorithms implemented in the superclass through
inheritance. The superclass forces the subclass to implement certain methods.

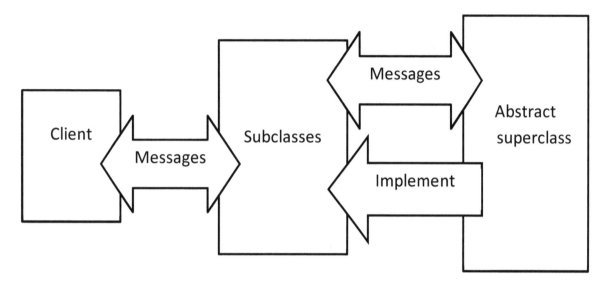

Abstraction process: The process of abstraction lies in determining the data structure and the
hierarchical structure of classes that solve a problem. Given a hierarchical class structure,
attentive programmers can ask: Can it contain different algorithms to solve problems?

Java UML diagram for configuration 1.1 - variant 2: Many references, an object in memory by reference

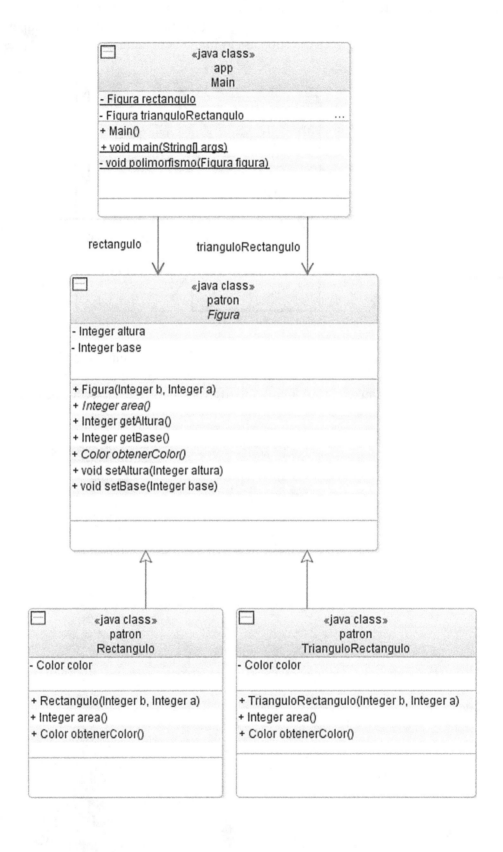

Source code for configuration 1.1 - variant 2

```java
package app;

import patron.Figura;
import patron.Rectangulo;
import patron.TrianguloRectangulo;

public class Main {
    public Main() {
        super(); //invoca el constructor de la superclase Object
    }
    //declarar todas las referencias de objetos que sean necesarias
    private static Figura rectangulo = null;
    private static Figura trianguloRectangulo = null;

    public static void main(String[] args) {
        Main main = new Main(); //el objeto main tiene información
relevante a la clase Main{}

        //esto es un error, no es posible crear instancias de una clase
abstracta
        //Figura figura = new Figura();

        System.out.println("Polimorfismo dinámico o de referencia");
        System.out.println("Muchas referencias un objeto por referencia
en memoria");

        //crear un objeto para cada referencia
        rectangulo = new Rectangulo(6, 8);
        polimorfismo(rectangulo);

        trianguloRectangulo = new TrianguloRectangulo(6, 8);
        polimorfismo(trianguloRectangulo);

    } //Fin del cuerpo del método main()

    //Método polimórfico o sobrecargado por el argumento del parámetro
    //El parámetro acepta tipos de argumentos distintos
    //En algunas ocasiones el argumento es del tipo rectángulo
    //  y en otras es del tipo triángulo rectángulo

    private static void polimorfismo(Figura figura) {

        //Líneas    polimórficas,    tienen    comportamiento    distintos
dependiendo de la figura
```

```
        //La JVM Java decide que comportamiento ejecutar dependiendo del
tipo del argumento enviado en el parámetro

        System.out.println(figura.getClass().getName());
        System.out.println("  Altura = " + figura.getAltura());
        System.out.println("  Base = " + figura.getBase());
        System.out.println("  Área " + figura.area());
        System.out.println("  Color " + figura.obtenerColor());


    } //Fin del cuerpo del método polimórfico

} //Fin del cuerpo de la clase Main{}
```

Summary of the topics discussed so far

The configuration 1.1 in variant 1, declares a reference and an object instance, the only reference is pointed to a new object instance whenever it is needed. The memory usage is small but the JVM must collect instances of non-referenced objects.

The configuration 1.1 in variant 2, declares many references and an object instance for each reference, each reference is pointed to an object instance. The use of memory is greater because of the large number of objects in memory. The JVM has little work, since it should not collect unreferenced objects.

Structure of knowledge learned so far. Programming with polymorphism:
- Establish the data structure (abstraction: group the "Use Cases")
- Establish the hierarchical structure of classes (abstraction: relationships, inheritance)
- Determine a design pattern (layered structure)
    - o Determine the algorithms (procedural or practical)
        - Specialized algorithms that solve the problem (suppliers)
        - Polymorphic algorithms that use the solution found (clients)
            - Static polymorphism (parameter overload)
            - Dynamic polymorphism (overload of the arguments)

Note: In configuration 1.1 variant 2, the modifications of the source code have been made in the class that has the client role. The classes that have the role of suppliers have not had changes in the code and have remained the same as the configuration 1.1 variant 1.

Explanation of the most relevant lines of code in configuration 1.1 - variant 2

Only the source code of the class with the client role will be explained: Main{}. The rest of the source code is identical to the configuration 1.1 variant 1.

```
package app;

import patron.Figura;
import patron.Rectangulo;
import patron.TrianguloRectangulo;

public class Main {
    public Main() {
        super(); //invoca el constructor de la superclase Object
    }
```

In variant number two, you must create the same number of references of objects and instances of objects to solve the problem.

```
    //declarar todas las referencias de objetos que sean necesarias
    private static Figura rectangulo = null;
    private static Figura trianguloRectangulo = null;
```

```
    public static void main(String[] args) {
        Main main = new Main(); //el objeto main tiene información
relevante a la clase Main{}

        //esto es un error, no es posible crear instancias de una clase
abstracta
        //Figura figura = new Figura();

        System.out.println("Polimorfismo dinámico o de referencia");
        System.out.println("Muchas referencias un objeto por referencia
en memoria");
```

For each reference you have to create an object instance, there are as many objects as references have been created. If the JVM finds an unreferenced object, it will clear it from memory. Variant number two tries to reduce the work of the JVM by keeping all the objects with their corresponding reference throughout the execution of the application.

```
        //crear un objeto para cada referencia
        rectangulo = new Rectangulo(6, 8);
        polimorfismo(rectangulo);

        trianguloRectangulo = new TrianguloRectangulo(6, 8);
        polimorfismo(trianguloRectangulo);

    } //Fin del cuerpo del método main()
```

The JVM will evaluate the method argument at run time: `private static void polimorfismo(Figura figura) {...}`, to decide which method to execute given the object instance called `figura`, for example: `figura.getAltura();`

```
//Método polimórfico o sobrecargado por el argumento del parámetro
//El parámetro acepta tipos de argumentos distintos
//En algunas ocasiones el argumento es del tipo rectángulo
//  y en otras es del tipo triángulo rectángulo
private static void polimorfismo(Figura figura) {
    //Líneas polimórficas, tienen comportamiento distinto dependiendo
de la figura
    //La JVM Java decide que comportamiento ejecutar dependiendo del
tipo del argumento enviado en el parámetro
    System.out.println(figura.getClass().getName());
    System.out.println("  Altura = " + figura.getAltura());
    System.out.println("  Base = " + figura.getBase());
    System.out.println("  Área " + figura.area());
    System.out.println("  Color " + figura.obtenerColor());

} //Fin del cuerpo del método polimórfico

} //Fin del cuerpo de la clase Main{}
```

Summary of important topics discussed so far

The creation of polymorphic methods allows the JVM to decide which method to execute, depending on the type of argument and the type of parameter. Polymorphic methods fulfill two objectives of object-oriented programming.

Objective of object-oriented programming:
1. Reduction of the amount of code written by the programmers. In this case, a line of code has been written that executes two behaviors. For example: `figura.getAltura();` is executed for the calculation of the area of two different figures.
2. Creation of reusable modules. In this case, the method called `polimorfismo()` has been used to reuse it in the calculation of the area of a quadrilateral and in the calculation of the area of a right triangle. Also the design pattern can be reused with different polymorphic algorithms, for example: "do not print the color if the area is less than 100".

The polymorphism mechanism allows to reduce the code written by the programmers and create reusable modules. An astute programmer will always find a way to write little code and let the JVM have to do as much work as possible when solving a problem.

Configuration 1.2 - References of objects and objects are created using the subclasses

In configuration 1.2, a new constraint is established, it is not feasible to create references from the superclass. In this configuration there are two restrictions: do not create objects of the superclass and do not create references of the superclass.

In configuration 1.2, references and objects are created from subclasses.

Java code to create the configuration 1.2

```
SubClase01 objeto01 = null;   //crear una referencia usando la subclase
Objeto01 = new SubClase01(); //apuntar la referencia a un nuevo objeto

SubClase02 objeto02 = null;   //crear una referencia usando la subclase
Objeto02 = new SubClase02(); //apuntar la referencia a un nuevo objeto

SubClase03 objeto03 = null;   //crear una referencia usando la subclase
Objeto03 = new SubClase03(); //apuntar la referencia a un nuevo objeto

SubClaseN objetoN = null;   //crear una referencia usando la subclase
ObjetoN = new SubClaseN(); //apuntar la referencia a un nuevo objeto
```

Properties of configuration 1.2

	Create references	Create objects
Superclass (abstract)	X (restriction)	Not allowed
Subclass	Yes	Yes

Utility of configuration 1.2

It is a suitable configuration for when there are few specialized objects, each object has the need to implement a particular or unique algorithm. If so many references are declared as specialized objects it is possible to have in memory all the objects that are needed to solve a problem. Each reference works as a pointer to each specialized object. Objects can remain in memory during the entire execution time of the application.

A static assignment means that the reference and the object instance are made with the same class. The compiler can easily deduce, at design time, the type of object declared in a parameter of a method. In a static assignment the parameter and the arguments are of the same type.

The static assignment of each reference to an object allows applying the static polymorphism mechanism, each reference can send messages to a specialized object. If all subclasses implement a single interface, they can receive identical messages from the references.

To apply or use the static polymorphism mechanism you need to send messages to the objects through a method interface. Each object must implement the same methods interface.

The declaration of abstract methods in the superclass specifies a contract that subclasses must respect. Subclasses will comply with the contract when they implement the missing code. The declaration of non-abstract methods in the superclass specifies an optional contract that subclasses could meet or not comply with.

The abstract classes declare two types of methods:
  1. Methods with code in the body. Classes that inherit an abstract class may optionally overwrite these methods.
  2. Methods without code or without body. Classes that inherit an abstract class must overwrite these methods; implementing the missing code.

The methods declared as abstract are widely used by systems analysts to specify user requirements during the process of building a software product.

The process of abstraction is a psychological process that a human performs to find the solution to a problem. Classes and abstract methods are tools that information systems analysts use to specify the solution to a problem. The programmers interpret the specifications indicated by the information systems analysts and write the missing or specified code.

Java UML diagram for configuration 1.2

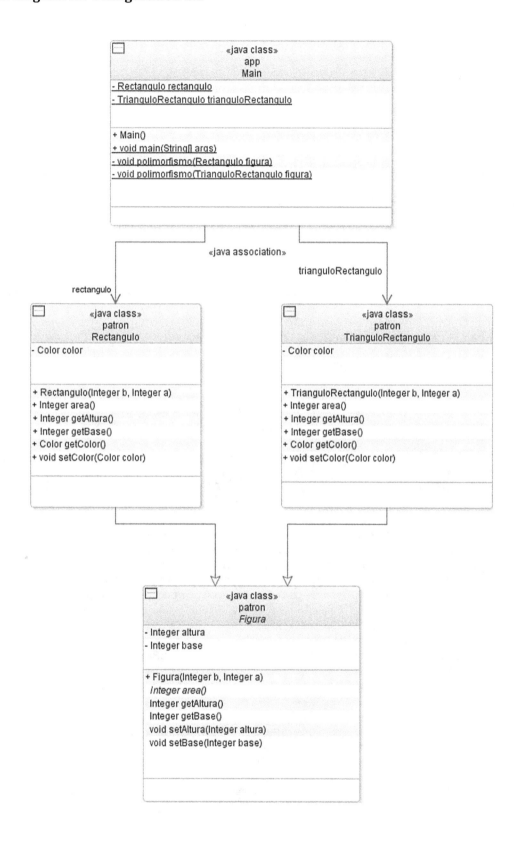

Código fuente para la configuración 1.2

```java
package app;
import patron.Rectangulo;
import patron.TrianguloRectangulo;
public class Main {
    public Main() {
        super();
    }
    private static Rectangulo rectangulo  = null;
    private static TrianguloRectangulo trianguloRectangulo = null;

    //Esta línea es un error, la clase Figura{} no es pública
    //La clase Figura{} está protegida en el paquete patron
    //private static Figura figura = null;

    public static void main(String[] args) {
        Main main = new Main();
        System.out.println("Polimorfismo  por  sobrecarga  del  parámetro  del
método");
        rectangulo = new Rectangulo(3, 4);
        polimorfismo(rectangulo);
        trianguloRectangulo = new TrianguloRectangulo(5, 4);
        polimorfismo(trianguloRectangulo);

        //Esta línea es un error, la clase Figura{} no es pública
        //La clase Figura{} está protegida en el paquete patron
        //Figura figura = new Rectangulo(2,4);

        //Esto  es  un  error,  no  es  posible  crear  instancias  de  una  clase
abstracta
        //Figura figura = new Figura();

    }
    //El compilador Java decide que método ejecutar en tiempo de ejecución
    //Método polimórfico o sobrecargado por el parámetro
    private static void polimorfismo(Rectangulo figura) {
        //Líneas no polimórficas, siempre se comportan como un rectángulo
        //El compilador Java decide que comportamiento ejecutar en tiempo de
diseño
        System.out.println(figura.getClass().getName());
        System.out.println("   Altura = " + figura.getAltura());
        System.out.println("   Base = " + figura.getBase());
        System.out.println("   Área " + figura.area());
        System.out.println("   Color " + figura.getColor());
    }

    //Método polimórfico o sobrecargado por el parámetro

    private static void polimorfismo(TrianguloRectangulo figura) {

        //Líneas  no  polimórficas,  siempre  se  comportan  como  un  triángulo
rectángulo
        //El compilador Java decide que comportamiento ejecutar en tiempo de
diseño

        System.out.println(figura.getClass().getName());
        System.out.println("   Altura = " + figura.getAltura());
```

```
        System.out.println("  Base = " + figura.getBase());
        System.out.println("  Área " + figura.area());
        System.out.println("  Color " + figura.getColor());
    }
}

package patron;
import java.awt.Color;
public final class Rectangulo extends Figura {
    private Color color = new Color(0, 0, 0);
    public void setColor(Color color) {
        this.color = color;
    }

    public Color getColor() {
        return color;
    }
    public Rectangulo(Integer b, Integer a) {
        super(b, a);
        color = Color.orange;
    }
    @Override
    public Integer area() {
        return this.getAltura() * this.getBase();
    }
    @Override
    public Integer getAltura() {
        // TODO Implement this method
        return super.getAltura();
    }
    @Override
    public Integer getBase() {
        // TODO Implement this method
        return super.getBase();
    }
}

package patron;
import java.awt.Color;
public final class TrianguloRectangulo extends Figura {
    private Color color = new Color(0, 0, 0);
    public void setColor(Color color) {
        this.color = color;
    }
    public Color getColor() {
        return color;
    }
    public TrianguloRectangulo(Integer b, Integer a) {
        super(b, a);
        color = Color.green;
    }
    @Override
    public Integer area() {
        return (this.getAltura() * this.getBase()) / 2;
```

```
    }
    @Override
    public Integer getAltura() {
        // TODO Implement this method
        return super.getAltura();
    }
    @Override
    public Integer getBase() {
        // TODO Implement this method
        return super.getBase();
    }
}

package patron;

//Los niveles de control de acceso protected y por defecto para miembros.

//  Un miembro default puede ser accedido solo si la clase que
//    accede al miembro pertenece al mismo paquete.
//  Un miembro protected puede ser accedido por la herencia,
//    la subclase puede pertenecer al mismo paquete u otro paquete.
//Los niveles de control de acceso public y por defecto para clases.
//  Una clase pública puede ser accedida por cualquier clase de cualquier
paquete.
//  Una clase sin modificador puede ser accedida por una clase de su
mismo paquete

abstract class Figura {
    private Integer altura = 0;
    private Integer base = 0;

    public Figura(Integer b, Integer a) {
        base = b;
        altura = a;
        //super();
    }
    protected void setAltura(Integer altura) {
        this.altura = altura;
    }
    protected void setBase(Integer base) {
        this.base = base;
    }
    protected Integer getAltura() {
        return altura;
    }
    protected Integer getBase() {
        return base;
    }
    protected abstract Integer area();
}
```

Explanation of the most relevant lines of code in configuration 1.2

Comments will be made on the most interesting aspects of the lines of code; many lines of code have been discussed above.

```
package app;
```

The following lines of code import the classes from the package called `patron`. The package called `patron` will contain the classes of the layer called `proveedor`. An interesting aspect of the 1.2 configuration is that it is not necessary to access the class called `Figura{}`. The class with the name of `Figura{}` must be encapsulated in the package called `patron`. To encapsulate a class in a package, you must use the default modifier in the declaration of the name of the class.

```
import patron.Rectangulo;
import patron.TrianguloRectangulo;
```

```
public class Main {
    public Main() {
        super();//es una buena costumbre ejecutar el constructor de la
superclase, toda clase hereda por defecto a la clase Object
    }
```

These lines of code are the declaration of the references to the subclasses, the references are not pointing to any object. The configuration 1.2 does not need to access the class `Figura{}`, for this reason, the class `Figure{}` has been declared non-public in the `proveedor` layer.

```
    private static Rectangulo rectangulo  = null;
    private static TrianguloRectangulo trianguloRectangulo = null;

    //Esta línea es un error, la clase Figura{} no es pública
    //La clase Figura{} está protegida en el paquete patron
    //private static Figura figura = null;

    public static void main(String[] args) {
        Main main = new Main(); //el objeto main tiene información relevante
a la clase Main{}

        System.out.println("Polimorfismo por sobrecarga del parámetro del
método");

        rectangulo = new Rectangulo(3, 4);
```

Execution of the static polymorphic method called polymorphism (). The parameter and the argument are of the same type, in this case it is of the rectangle type.

```
        polimorfismo(rectangulo);

        trianguloRectangulo = new TrianguloRectangulo(5, 4);
```

Execution of the static polymorphic method called polymorphism (). The parameter and the argument are of the same type; in this case it is of the right triangle type.

```
    polimorfismo(trianguloRectangulo);

        //Esta línea es un error, la clase Figura{} no es pública
        //La clase Figura{} está protegida en el paquete patron
        //Figura figura = new Rectangulo(2,4);

        //Esto  es  un  error  por  dos  motivos:  no  es  posible  crear
instancias  de  una  clase  abstracta  ni  se  puede  tener  acceso  a  clases
protegidas en el paquete
        //Figura figura = new Figura();

    } //Fin del cuerpo del método main()
```

The following code implements the declaration of the two static polymorphic methods necessary to solve the area calculation problem. The two methods have the same name: polymorphism (...). The two methods are differentiated by the type of parameter.

Static polymorphic methods are characterized by having parameters and arguments of the same type. The parameter and the argument are of the type: 1) rectangle, 2) right triangle.

Static polymorphic methods implement static polymorphic algorithms. Static polymorphic algorithms invoke different behaviors using the same message. For example: `figura.getAltura();`

Static polymorphic methods send messages to classes that have the role of providing the desired behaviors. Classes that are clients implement static polymorphic algorithms. The classes that are providers implement specialized behavior algorithms.

The main characteristic of static polymorphic algorithms is that the behavior and messages sent are defined at the design time of the Java application.

```
    //El compilador Java decide que método ejecutar en tiempo de diseño
según su parámetro.
    //Método polimórfico o sobrecargado por el parámetro.

    private static void polimorfismo(Rectangulo figura) {

        //Líneas  polimórficas  estáticas,  siempre  se  comportan  como  un
rectángulo.
        //El compilador Java decide que comportamiento ejecutar en tiempo
de diseño.

        System.out.println(figura.getClass().getName());
        System.out.println("  Altura = " + figura.getAltura());
        System.out.println("  Base = " + figura.getBase());
        System.out.println("  Área " + figura.area());
        System.out.println("  Color " + figura.getColor());

    }//Fin del cuerpo del método polimórfico
```

```
    //El compilador Java decide que método ejecutar en tiempo de diseño
según su parámetro
    //Método polimórfico o sobrecargado por el parámetro.

    private static void polimorfismo(TrianguloRectangulo figura) {

        //Líneas polimórficas estáticas, siempre se comportan como un
triángulo rectángulo.
        //El compilador Java decide que comportamiento ejecutar en tiempo
de diseño.

        System.out.println(figura.getClass().getName());
        System.out.println("  Altura = " + figura.getAltura());
        System.out.println("  Base = " + figura.getBase());
        System.out.println("  Área " + figura.area());
        System.out.println("  Color " + figura.getColor());

    }//Fin del cuerpo del método polimórfico

}//Fin del cuerpo de la clase Main{}
```

Summary of concepts:
- A method is polymorphic if it is overloaded in its parameters or arguments or both.
- An algorithm is polymorphic if it sends the same message to the classes supplying the specialized behaviors. In this case, the class with the client role sends the `getAltura()`, `getBase()`, `area()` and `getColor()` messages to the supplying classes of these behaviors.
- Classes that are clients implement polymorphic methods and algorithms. Polymorphic algorithms send messages to classes that provide specialized behavior.
- The classes that have the role of providers implement a single methods interface to receive messages from the classes that have the role of clients.

The following classes belong to the package with the name of "`patron`". These classes will provide specific behaviors.

Many of these lines of code have already been commented, the most relevant aspects will be discussed.

```
package patron;
```

The following lines of code declare the class called `Figura{}`, the class called `Figura{}` is declared without the access modifier, the default access modifier indicates that the class is protected in the package that contains it.

Access modifiers for fields of a class:
1. `public`: any class has access to the field (not recommended)
2. `private`: no class has access to the field (recommended)
3. `protected`: the classes of the same package and the classes that inherit the fields can access said fields, the classes that are heirs and those that are inherited can be in different packages (only when necessary)

4. without modifier: the field that has the default modifier is accessed by the classes that belong to the same package (only when necessary)

Access modifiers for classes:
1. `public`: public classes can be accessed from any package (only when necessary)
2. without modifier: a class declared without a modifier is accessed by the classes of its same package or from another package through inheritance (recommended)

The `abstract` modifier for methods and classes:
- If a method is declared abstract it can not have Java code implemented, if a class has an abstract method then the class must also be declared abstract. It is not feasible to instantiate objects of an abstract class. The missing Java code should be implemented by the class that is related through the inheritance with the abstract class.
- If a class is declared abstract, it will not be possible to instantiate objects from it, regardless of whether it has an abstract method declared or not. The only way to access an abstract class is through inheritance. The `abstract` modifier is incompatible with the `final` modifier. The `final` modifier is used to prevent a class from being inherited by another class.

```
//Los niveles de control de acceso protected y por defecto para miembros
  de una clase:
//   Un miembro default puede ser accedido sólo si la clase que
//      accede al miembro de la clase pertenece al mismo paquete.
//   Un miembro declarado como protected puede ser accedido por la
  herencia, la subclase puede pertenecer al mismo paquete u otro paquete.
//Los niveles de control de acceso public y por defecto para clases:
//   Una clase pública puede ser accedida por cualquier clase de cualquier
  paquete
//   Una clase sin modificador puede ser accedida por una clase de su
  mismo paquete o desde otro paquete a través de la herencia

abstract class Figura {

    private Integer altura = 0;
    private Integer base = 0;
```

The following code is the declaration of the constructor method called `Figura()`, the method called `Figura()` must be public and homonymous to the class called `Figura{}`. It is a good idea to use the constructor method to initialize the fields in the class. The constructor method is the primary interface for accessing the private data of the class. If a class is abstract its constructor method can be invoked by the class that inherits it.

```
    public Figura(Integer b, Integer a) {
        base = b;
        altura = a;
        //super();//No es necesario invocar el constructor de una superclase
    }
```

The following lines of codes are the declaration of the interface of private data access methods of the class. If a method is declared without a modifier, only the classes of its same package can access the method. The methods can have four modifiers:

1. without modifier: only the classes in the same package access the method
2. `protected`: only the classes of the same package access the method and the classes that inherit the method, the classes that inherit the method can be in another package
3. `public`: all classes can access the method
4. `private`: no class can access the method, only the class itself can access the method

```
void setAltura(Integer altura) {
    this.altura = altura;
}

void setBase(Integer base) {
    this.base = base;
}

integer getAltura() {
    return altura;
}

integer getBase() {
    return base;
}
```

The next line of code is the declaration of the interface of abstract methods, there will be as many methods called area () as there are subclasses. Abstract methods must be overwritten by the class that inherits this class. If a method is declared without the access modifier, then only the classes in the same package can access the method.

Important note and a fascinating detail about polymorphism in Java: You have to understand that a line of code has been written, and it is correct to say: "interface of abstract methods". In the future, the classes that have the role of clients will be able to create many objects of different types, each type of object will implement a different version of the method called `area()`.

```
    abstract Integer area();//Declaración de la: "interfaz de métodos
abstractos"

}//Fin del cuerpo de la clase Figura{}
```

This line of code indicates that the class `Rectangulo{}` belongs to the package called `patron`, the package with the name of `patron` will contain the classes of the layer called `proveedor`.

```
package patron;
```

```
import java.awt.Color;
```

The following line of code is the declaration of the class called `Rectangulo{}`, it is a public class since it will be invoked from the package with the name of **app**. The `Rectangulo{}` class is extended from the class called `Figura{}` and inherits the public methods interface to access the private data of the `Figura{}` class. The **final** modifier indicates that the class `Rectangulo{}` can not be inherited by another class, programmers must necessarily instantiate an object of the class `Rectangulo{}`.

```
public final class Rectangulo extends Figura {

    private Color color = new Color(0, 0, 0);

    public Rectangulo(Integer b, Integer a) {
        super(b, a); //Ejecutar el constructor de la superclase. Acceder
a la estructura de datos de la superclase
        color = Color.orange;
    }

    public void setColor(Color color) {
        this.color = color;
    }

    public Color getColor() {
        return color;
    }
```

The following lines of code overwrite the abstract methods inherited from the superclass. The method that is overwritten will implement the specialized or more specific code than the code implemented in the superclass. Each subclass will implement a more specialized or more specific code version. Normally, superclasses implement a code of a higher level of abstraction, and subclasses implement a code of a greater level of concretion or specialization. It is also advisable to implement in the superclass the code that all subclasses need. If there is a subclass that needs exclusive code, it would be better if those classes take over the exclusive code. When subclasses need to implement a unique code, the superclass will declare a method with the abstract modifier. If subclasses need to execute shared code, then the superclass will implement methods with code in its body.

```
    @Override
    public Integer area() {
        //implementar el código faltante en la superclase
        //implementación del código especializado o de mayor concreción
        return this.getAltura() * this.getBase();

    }

    @Override
    public Integer getAltura() {
        // TODO Implement this method
        //ejecutar el código de mayor abstracción, implementado en la
superclase
        return super.getAltura();
    }

    @Override
    public Integer getBase() {
        // TODO Implement this method
        //ejecutar el código de mayor abstracción, implementado en la
superclase
        return super.getBase();
```

```
    }

}//Fin del cuerpo de la clase Rectangulo{}
```

Summary of the commented code

Characteristics of the code written in the superclass:
- The code implemented in the methods with body, not abstract, are methods that have a higher level of abstraction.
- Non-abstract methods are shared or used by all subclasses.
- The methods declared as abstract do not have code implemented, they have no body.
- If a method is declared as abstract, it means that the superclass gave up implementing a version of the method.
- The methods declared as abstract must be compulsorily overwritten in the subclasses.

Characteristics of the code in the subclasses:
- The code written in the methods is of a higher level of specification or specialization
- Subclasses are forced to overwrite the abstract methods of the superclass
- They can, optionally, overwrite the non-abstract methods of the superclass
- If the subclasses overwrite a non-abstract method, they are trying to:
  - Implement methods with new features
  - Implement a new version more concrete or with a lower level of abstraction
  - Implement a new version to completely replace the superclass code

Example of abstraction in the superclass: all the figures have sides, the quadrilaterals and the triangles that are rectangles have in common the base and the height.

Example of specialization in a subclass: the area of the quadrilateral is calculated specifically as follows: (base * altura)

Example of specialization in a subclass: the area of the triangle-rectangle is calculated specifically as follows: ((base * altura) / 2)

With respect to the color property of the figures, it is the responsibility of the analysts to decide if the color property will be implemented in the superclass or implemented in the subclasses. The process of abstraction is the task of deciding how the properties of the problem to be solved will be grouped. It will always be the responsibility of analysts and programmers to decide what level of abstraction a property of an object will have.

During the development process in the construction of a software product, analysts and programmers participate in the solution of a problem by separating or grouping the properties and procedures that give solution to the proposed problem.

The class hierarchy is a construction that helps to separate and group the properties and procedures that define the objects that participate in the solution of a problem. In a hierarchy of classes related by inheritance, the classes that have the role of being superclasses will implement the general or more abstract aspects of the problem to be solved. And the classes that have the role of being subclasses will implement the particular or more concrete aspects of the proposed solution.

The following graphic shows the concepts explained

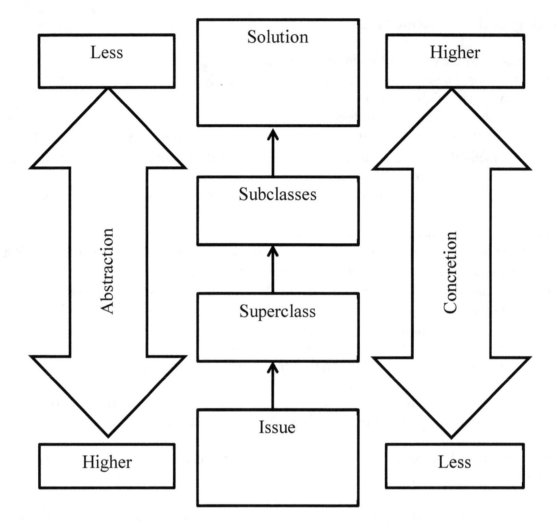

The following graph shows the relationship between the design pattern and polymorphic algorithms

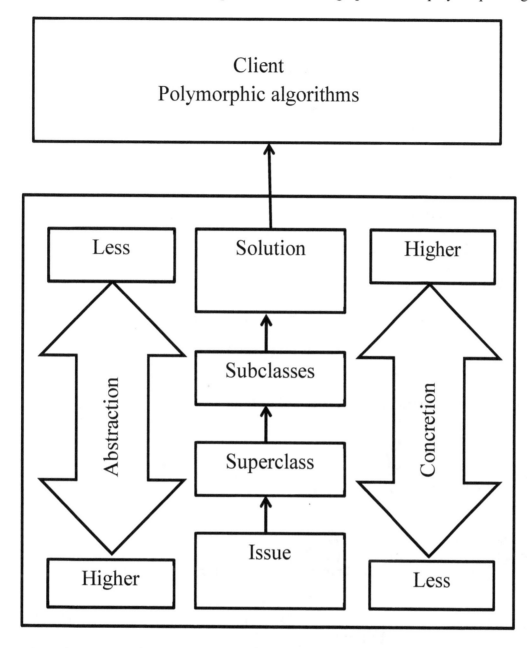

In object-oriented programming the concept of polymorphism can be used as a synonym of reuse, polymorphic algorithms are the different ways to use a solution, for example: if in a design pattern implements the solution of the movements of the characters of a game , the polymorphic algorithms will be the different ways of using the movements of the characters.

Note and detail to keep in mind: Some problems have solutions with a higher level of abstraction, for example: scientists who study distant galaxies look for general solutions that explain the cosmological processes.

The following lines of code implement a class with the name of: `TrianguloRectangulo{}`, the class belongs to the package called `patron`. The package called `patron` will contain the classes of the layer called the `proveedor`.

This class will implement the highest level of concretion for triangles that are rectangles. Details of higher abstraction level will be inherited from the class called `Figura{}`. It will also implement a public methods interface to offer the services that customers require. And will specialize in the calculation of triangles that are rectangles, customers will request these services by sending messages.

```java
package patron;

import java.awt.Color;

public final class TrianguloRectangulo extends Figura {

    private Color color = new Color(0, 0, 0);

    public TrianguloRectangulo(Integer b, Integer a) {
        super(b, a);
        color = Color.green;
    }

    public void setColor(Color color) {
        this.color = color;
    }

    public Color getColor() {
        return color;
    }


    @Override
    public Integer area() {
        return (this.getAltura() * this.getBase()) / 2;
    }

    @Override
    public Integer getAltura() {
        // TODO Implement this method
        return super.getAltura();
    }

    @Override
    public Integer getBase() {
        // TODO Implement this method
        return super.getBase();
    }

}//Fin del cuerpo de la clase TrianguloRectangulo{}
```

Group number two of configurations

In the group of configurations number two, the subclasses are declared with the modifier: `abstract`. The configuration of subclasses declared as abstract is not recommended. Surely some particular problems need this type of configuration.

In group two there are two possibilities to use the design pattern:
- Possibility 1: inherit the abstract subclasses of the design pattern (recommended)
- Possibility 2: declare references to instances of objects and instances of objects using the superclass (not recommended)

In possibility number two: it is not possible to apply the polymorphism mechanism; it is not feasible to differentiate the types of objects.

Declaring subclasses as abstract classes is an exceptional situation and will largely depend on the problem to be solved. It is advisable to try, in a first instance, to declare the superclass with the abstract class modifier.

What happens if subclasses are declared with the abstract class modifier?

When declaring a subclass with the abstract class modifier, a very large constraint is imposed and the Java compiler will give errors every time an object of an abstract subclass is built. Remember that it is not feasible to instantiate objects from an abstract class.

Properties of configuration 2

	Create references	Create objects	
Superclass	Yes	Yes	It does not have much use
Subclass (`abstract`)	Yes	Not allowed	Compiler error (Inherit the design pattern to skip the errors)

Classes that have the customer role of the design pattern can not use the design pattern effectively. It is advisable that the classes that have the customer role of the design pattern inherit the design pattern.

Many of the following lines of Java code would generate compiler errors at design time.

```
package app;

import patron.Figura;
import patron.Rectangulo;
import patron.TrianguloRectangulo;

public class Main {

    //Esto no es un error: el compilador podrá crear referencias de clases
    abstractas y no abstractas sin problema
    //El problema radica, más tarde, al momento de crear los objetos de clases
    abstractas con sus respectivos métodos constructores
    private static Figura figura = null;
    private static Rectangulo rectangulo = null;
    private static TrianguloRectangulo trianguloRectangulo = null;
```

```
    public Main() {
        super();
    }

    public static void main(String[] args) {
        Main main = new Main();

        /////////////////////////////////////
        //Esto no es un error
        //No tiene mucha utilidad crear referencias y objetos de una superclase
        figura = new Figura();

        //Error: no es factible crear objetos de clases abstractas
        figura = new Rectangulo();

        //Error: no es factible crear objetos de clases abstractas
        figura = new TrianguloRectangulo();

        /////////////////////////////////////
        //Error de tipos: no se puede crear referencias de una subclase y
objetos de una superclase
        //Siempre la referencia y el objeto construido deben ser del mismo tipo
        rectangulo = new Figura();

        //Error de tipos: no se puede crear referencias de un tipo y objetos de
otro tipo
        //Siempre la referencia y el objeto construido deben ser del mismo tipo
        //Error: no es factible crear objetos de clases abstractas
        rectangulo = new TrianguloRectangulo();

        //Error: no es factible crear objetos de clases abstractas
        rectangulo = new Rectangulo();

        /////////////////////////////////////
        //Error de tipos: no se puede crear referencias de una subclase y
objetos de una superclase
        //Siempre la referencia y el objeto construido deben ser del mismo tipo
        trianguloRectangulo = new Figura();

        //Error de tipos: no se puede crear referencias de un tipo y objetos de
otro tipo
        //Siempre la referencia y el objeto construido deben ser del mismo tipo
        //Error: no es factible crear objetos de clases abstractas
        trianguloRectangulo = new Rectangulo();

        //Error: no es factible crear objetos de clases abstractas
        trianguloRectangulo = new TrianguloRectangulo();

    }
}
```

Solution to the problems presented by the subclasses that are declared as abstract

The solution is to inherit the subclasses of the design pattern from the classes that have the customer role. Classes that have the role of client must inherit the design pattern.

The following Java class diagram and the Java code associated with that diagram show how to inherit a design pattern. The code will not be commented, it was commented in the previous examples. It is recommended that the programmer write the code in their favorite IDE.

The secret lies in understanding that two new classes have been created that serve as a bridge between the class that is the client and the design pattern.

Diagram of Java classes in UML - Configuration 2, possibility 1 (Inherit a pattern)

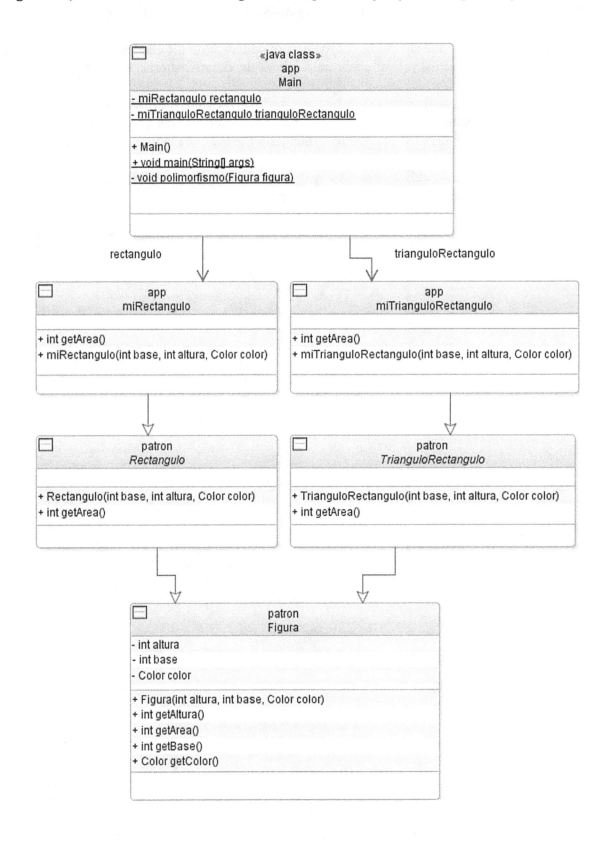

Source code of configuration 2, possibility 1 (Inherit a pattern)

```java
package app;

import java.awt.Color;

import patron.Figura;

//Clase cliente del patrón de diseño
public class Main {

    //Declaración de las referencias
    private static miRectangulo rectangulo = null;
    private static miTrianguloRectangulo trianguloRectangulo= null;

    public Main() {
        super();
    }

    public static void main(String[] args) {
        Main main = new Main();

        //Apuntar la referencia a un nuevo objeto
        rectangulo = new miRectangulo(3, 4, new Color(128, 128, 128));

        //Invocar al método polimórfico con el argumento del tipo
rectángulo
        polimorfismo(rectangulo);

        //Apuntar la referencia a un nuevo objeto
        trianguloRectangulo =    new miTrianguloRectangulo(5,  6,  new
Color(128, 128, 128));

        //Invocar al método polimórfico con el argumento del tipo
triángulo rectángulo
        polimorfismo(trianguloRectangulo);

    }

    //Este método es polimórfico por sobrecarga del argumento en el
parámetro
    private static void polimorfismo(Figura figura) {
        //Este algoritmo es polimórfico ya que su comportamiento
depende del argumento en el parámetro
        //La JVM en tiempo de ejecución decidirá qué método ejecutará
dependiendo del tipo de argumento
        System.out.println("Tipo:    "  +  figura.getClass().getName());
//obtener el tipo
        System.out.println("  Base: " + figura.getBase());
        System.out.println("  Altura: " + figura.getAltura());
        System.out.println("  Color: " + figura.getColor());
        System.out.println("  Área: " + figura.getArea());
    }
```

```
}

package app;

import java.awt.Color;

import patron.Rectangulo;

//Clase puente a una clase abstracta
public class miRectangulo extends Rectangulo {

    public miRectangulo(int base, int altura, Color color) {
        super(base, altura, color);
    }

    //Sobrescribir los métodos a especializar o renunciados por la
superclase
    @Override
    public int getArea() {
        // TODO Implement this method
        //Implementar código especializado o de mayor nivel de concreción
        //Si no se desea implementar nuevo código, invocar el código
implementado en la superclase
        return super.getArea();
    }
```

```
}

package app;

import java.awt.Color;

import patron.TrianguloRectangulo;

//Clase puente a una clase abstracta
public class miTrianguloRectangulo extends TrianguloRectangulo {

    public miTrianguloRectangulo(int base, int altura, Color color) {
        super(base, altura, color);
    }

    //Sobrescribir los métodos a especializar o renunciados por la
superclase
    @Override
    public int getArea() {
        // TODO Implement this method
        //Implementar código especializado o de mayor nivel de concreción
        //Si no se desea implementar nuevo código, invocar el código
implementado en la superclase
        return super.getArea();
    }

}
```

```
package patron;

import java.awt.Color;

//Esta clase es accedida por las clases clientes en tiempo de diseño
//Esta clase es accedida por las subclases en tiempo de ejecución
public class Figura {
    //estructura de datos de mayor nivel de abstracción, datos en común
para todas las figuras
    private int altura = 0, base = 0;
    private Color color = null;

    //interfaz de construcción de objetos
    public Figura(int altura, int base, Color color) {
        super();
        this.altura = altura;
        this.base = base;
        this.color = color;
    }

    //Los siguientes métodos tienen acceso a la estructura de datos
    public int getAltura() {
        return altura;
    }

    public int getBase() {
        return base;
    }

    public Color getColor() {
        return color;
    }
    //Este método será sobrescrito en las subclases
    public int getArea() {
        //Las subclases, especializadas, se harán cargo del cálculo del
área para cada tipo de figura
        return 0; //Yo renuncio a implementar el cálculo del área de las
figuras
    }
}

package patron;

import java.awt.Color;

//Una clase abstracta puede tener o no tener métodos abstractos
public abstract class Rectangulo extends Figura {

    public Rectangulo(int base, int altura, Color color) {
        super(base, altura, color);
    }

    //Sobrescribir los métodos a especializar o renunciados por la
superclase
```

```
        @Override
    public int getArea() {
        // TODO Implement this method

        //Implementar código especializado o de mayor nivel de concreción

        return super.getBase() * super.getAltura();
    }
}

package patron;

import java.awt.Color;

//Una clase abstracta puede tener o no tener métodos abstractos
public abstract class TrianguloRectangulo extends Figura {

    public TrianguloRectangulo(int base, int altura, Color color) {
        super(base, altura, color);
    }

    //Sobrescribir los métodos a especializar o renunciados por la
superclase
    @Override
    public int getArea() {
        // TODO Implement this method

        //Implementar código especializado o de mayor nivel de concreción

        return (super.getBase() * super.getAltura()) / 2;
    }

}
```

End of chapter I - "How to use abstract classes in class inheritance"

Summary of the most important topics of Chapter I

What role do declarations of abstract methods fulfill in a superclass?

The declarations of abstract methods in the superclasses are contracts that the subclasses must respect and implement in Java code. When a superclass declares abstract methods the subclasses are forced to overwrite and implement the abstract methods.

What happens if a subclass waives the contract and does not overwrite the abstract methods?

The subclass can not resign, it must over write the abstract methods.

What happens if a subclass overwrites the abstract method, but waives the implementation of the missing code?

Yes, the subclass can resign. The missing code will be waiting for another class to implement it.

There are three types of relationships between classes in Java:
1. Inheritance: using the keyword "`extends`", is when a class is extended from another class. (It is an extension relationship between classes).
2. Has: using the keyword "`new`", is when a class creates an instance of object using the constructor method of another class. (Relation of belonging, a class has an object instance)
3. It is part: using the keyword "`interface`" is when a class is part of another class. (Composition ratio).

The topic of classes that are interfaces will be discussed in Chapter II.

In any of the three types of relationships, it is possible to overwrite the methods.

This is an example where a method has been overwritten in the creation of an object instance:

```
        unaFigura = new Rectangulo(6, 8){
            @Override
            public Integer area() {
                // TODO Implement this method
                //return  super.area();  //renunciar  al  código  de  la
subclase
                //Implementar nuevo código
                return this.getAltura() * this.getBase();
            }
        };
```

What does it mean to overwrite a method?

It will always involve specializing or raising the level of concreteness of a solution to a problem posed. It is optional to write or not write Java code in the body of an overwritten method.
- If the method is declared as abstract: the implementation of Java code will be left for later in the development of a software product.
- If the method is not abstract: The code implemented in the body of the method will be a new version of existing code.
- Overwriting a method will involve changes in:
  - The answer
  - The behavior

The importance of declaring the methods with the public access modifier: `public`

Overwriting public methods is an appropriate form of communication between classes that form inheritance trees. Message submissions are used to traverse hierarchical trees. The act of overwriting public methods is a way of relating classes by sending messages. The name of the method is the message; the arguments of the parameters are the content of the message. The responses of the message are the "`return`" of the method, and the algorithm implemented in the body of the method is the expected behavior. The expected behavior depends on the algorithm and the arguments of the parameters. By definition, the polymorphism is to achieve different behaviors, depending on the arguments of the parameter.

If the mechanism of the polymorphism has been applied correctly, then the implemented code has been reused. The reuse of code is one of the objectives of object-oriented programming.

Structure of a message statement		
Type of return or response	**Name of the method or message**	**Content of the message: are the arguments of the parameters**
`public Integer` `return (base * altura); //algoritmo o comportamiento` `}`	`areaRectangulo`	`(Integer base, Integer altura) {`

Classes that intend to receive messages must declare public methods; classes that implement public methods can receive messages and execute an algorithm depending on the content sent in the arguments of the parameter. To send a message it is necessary to instantiate an object of a class that has declared a structure of a message.

Example of sending a message:
```
NombreClasa objeto = new NombreClase();//crear un objeto
Integer respuesta = objeto.areaRectangulo(4, 5);//enviar un mensaje
System.out.println("Área = " + respuesta);//imprimir la respuesta
```

Description of the message:
- Type of response: An integer
- Message name: areaRectangulo
- Message content: base = 4, height = 5
- Message response: 20
- Expected behavior: calculate the area of a rectangle

The importance of the methods that are overwritten: When a class overwrites the methods of another class, it is trying to communicate with it to send messages and get an answer. The way to replace the response of a message is to overwrite the message and implement a new algorithm.

If a class is declared abstract, it must necessarily be inherited by another class in order to have the possibility of overwriting its abstract methods.

When overwriting methods that are abstract:
1. When the keyword is used: `extends` (relation: extension, inheritance)
2. When the keyword is used: `implements` (relation: aggregation)
3. When the keyword is used: `new` (relation: composition)

Methods that were not declared as abstract can also be overwritten using the `@Override` tag, it is not mandatory to overwrite non-abstract methods.

Chapter II

How to use the classes that are of type Interface in the inheritance relation between classes?

Group number three of configurations

In the group number three of configurations the superclasses implement the interface with prototypes of abstract methods, within this group there are two configurations. The number one configuration creates the object references using the superclasses and the creation of the objects using the subclasses. The second configuration creates the references of objects and objects using the subclasses.

This group has no restrictions, it is feasible to create references to objects and create objects using the constructors of the subclasses and superclass indistinctly.

The use of abstract classes have many restrictions compared to the use of interfaces, the use of interfaces allow greater flexibility when using the design pattern by the classes that have the role of clients.

Properties of group three:

	Create references	Create objects
Superclass (Interface)	Yes	Yes
Subclass	Yes	Yes

The configurations of this group form an adequate architecture to build a design pattern based on the inheritance relationship between classes.
1. Configuration 3.1: references are declared using superclasses. And the objects are declared using the subclasses.
2. Configuration 3.2: references and objects are declared using the subclasses.

What is an interface?

An interface is a special class that has all its methods declared as abstract. You can also declare, in the body of the interface, the fields that will be constant.

An interface, in Java, is a collection of abstract methods and constant fields.

Role of interfaces in the development of a software product:
- Specifies: What should be done to solve a problem?
- Does not specify: How to solve a problem?

The interfaces are used during the analysis phase in the development of a software product. The classes that implement these interfaces write the logic of the behavior of the abstract methods.

The use of Java interfaces provides the following advantages:
- Help in the process of abstraction in the process of analyzing the problem to be solved

- It allows to organize the system in modules.
- Establishes composition relationships between software parts. Classes can implement more than one interface per class.

Classes that implement one or more interfaces are obliged to overwrite all the methods declared in the interfaces.

Example of an interface declaration:

```
public abstract interface circulo {
    //superficie = pi * radio^2      //módulo de cálculo
    //perimetro = 2 * pi * radio     //módulo de cálculo
    public static float pi = 3.14f;  //campo constante
    public static float pi2 = 6.28f; //campo constante
    public    abstract    float    superficieCirculo(int    radio);    //método
    abstracto
    public    abstract    float    perimetroCirculo(int    radio);        //método
    abstracto
}

public abstract interface Figura {
    public static String tipoFigura = "anguloRecto"; //campo constant.
    public    abstract    int    calcularArea(int    base,    int    altura);    //método
    abstracto.
}
```

The following image shows the process of abstraction of the solution of a problem.

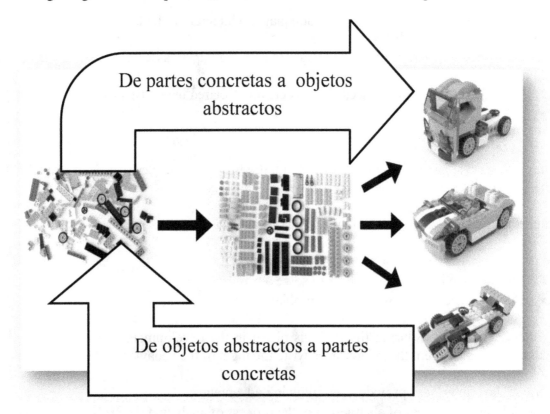

De partes concretas a objetos abstractos

De objetos abstractos a partes concretas

Analysts love the declarations of the interfaces, later the designers and the programmers will be obliged to implement the modules defined by the information systems analysts.

The interfaces are the highest level of abstraction possible in the process of building a software product, since they can specify the requirements of users. The eduction of user requirements is the first task to be performed. The designers and programmers should specify, later, the algorithms that solve the problems raised.

Configuration 3.1 - Creating the references of objects using the superclass and the creation of the objects using the subclasses.

In configuration 3.1, two constraints are introduced that force the architecture to function properly and also make good use of the design pattern based on inheritance between classes.

Properties of configuration 3.1

	Create references	**Create objects**
Superclass (Interface)	Yes	X(Restriction)
Subclass	X(Restriction)	Yes

This configuration has two variants:
3. Creating a reference using the superclass and many objects using the subclasses (consumes little memory, the garbage collector has a lot of work).
4. Creating many references using the superclass and an object for each reference using the subclasses (consumes more memory, the garbage collector has little work).

Characteristics of the configuration 3.1 - variant 1: a reference and many objects

Characteristics:
- A reference
- Many objects but only one object in memory
- Dynamic assignment of the reference to new objects
- Little memory consumption
- The JVM garbage collector has a lot of work cleaning the non-referenced objects

Java class diagram in UML for configuration 3.1 - variant 1: a reference and many objects

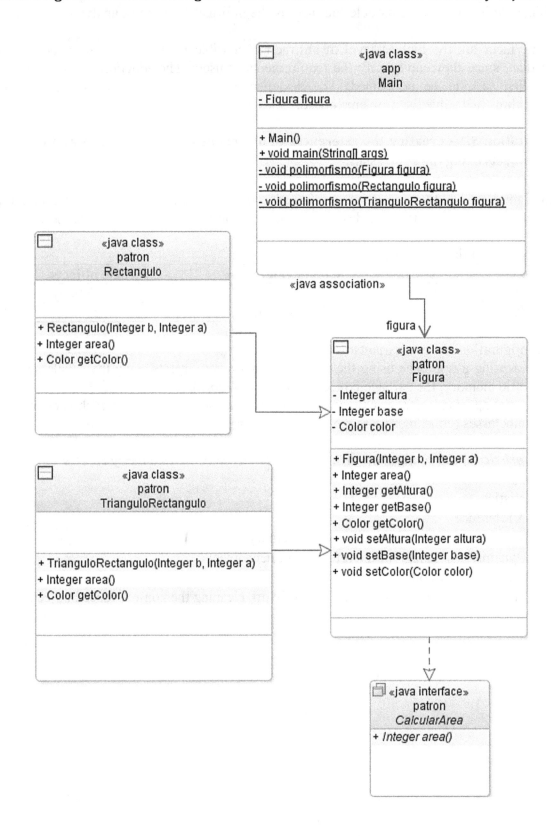

Source code for configuration 3.1 - variant 1

```
package app;

import patron.Figura;
import patron.Rectangulo;
import patron.TrianguloRectangulo;

public class Main {

    private static Figura figura = null;
    public Main() {
        super();
    }

    public static void main(String[] args) {
        Main main = new Main();

        System.out.println("Polimorfismo dinámico, una referencia muchos
objetos, con recolector de basura");

        figura = new Rectangulo(3, 4);
        polimorfismo(figura);
        figura = new TrianguloRectangulo(5, 4);
        polimorfismo(figura);
    }

    //Método polimórfico o sobrecargado por el argumento del parámetro
    //El parámetro acepta tipos de argumentos distintos
    //En algunas ocasiones el argumento es del tipo rectángulo
    //  y en otras es del tipo triángulo rectángulo

    private static void polimorfismo(Figura figura) {

        //Líneas polimórficas, tienen comportamiento distinto dependiendo
de la figura
        //El   compilador   Java   decide   que   comportamiento   ejecutar
dependiendo del tipo de argumento

        System.out.println(figura.getClass().getName());
        if(figura.area()>10)
          System.out.println("  Color = " + figura.getColor());
        System.out.println("  Altura = " + figura.getAltura());
        System.out.println("  Base = " + figura.getBase());
        System.out.println("  Área = " + figura.area());
    }

    private static void polimorfismo(Rectangulo figura) {
        //acceder a los métodos de Rectangulo{}, si es necesario

    }
    private static void polimorfismo(TrianguloRectangulo figura) {
        //acceder a los métodos de TrianguloRectangulo{}, si es necesario
```

```
    }

}//Fin del cuerpo de la clase Main{}

package patron;

public interface CalcularArea {

    //agregar todas las obligaciones de implementación para la clase
Figura{}

    public Integer area();
}

package patron;

import java.awt.Color;

public class Figura implements CalcularArea {
    private Integer altura = 0;
    private Integer base = 0;
    private Color color = null;

    public Figura(Integer b, Integer a) {
        base = b; altura = a;
        //super();
    }
    public void setAltura(Integer altura) {
        this.altura = altura;
    }

    public void setBase(Integer base) {
        this.base = base;
    }

    public Integer getAltura() {
        return altura;
    }

    public Integer getBase() {
        return base;
    }

    public void setColor(Color color) {
        this.color = color;
    }

    public Color getColor() {
        return color;
    }

    @Override
    public Integer area() {
```

```
if(this.getClass().getName().equalsIgnoreCase(Rectangulo.class.getName())
) {

            return altura * base;
        }else{
            return (altura * base) / 2;
        }

    }//fin del método abstracto sobrescrito

}//fin de la declaración de la clase Figura{}

package patron;

import java.awt.Color;

public class Rectangulo extends Figura {

    public Rectangulo(Integer b, Integer a) {

        super(b, a);//invocar al constructor de la clase Figura{}
        super.setColor(new    Color(Color.orange.getRGB()));//invocar    al
método setColor() de la clase Figura{}

    }

    /////////////////////////
    //sobrescribir todos los métodos de la clase Figura{} si es necesario
    /////////////////////////

    @Override
    public Color getColor() {
        // TODO Implement this method
        return super.getColor();
    }

    @Override
    public Integer area() {
        // TODO Implement this method
        //Opción 1: La clase Rectangulo{} implementa su propio
        //  algoritmo del cálculo del área
        //return super.getAltura() * super.getBase();

        //Opción 2: La clase Rectangulo{} invoca
        //  al algoritmo del cálculo del área de la superclase Figura{}
        return super.area();
    }
}

package patron;

import java.awt.Color;
```

```java
public class TrianguloRectangulo extends Figura {

    public TrianguloRectangulo(Integer b, Integer a) {
        super(b, a);
        super.setColor(new Color(Color.green.getRGB()));
    }

    /////////////////////////
    //sobrescribir todos los métodos de Figura si es necesario
    /////////////////////////

    @Override
    public Color getColor() {
        // TODO Implement this method
        return super.getColor();
    }

    @Override
    public Integer area() {

        // TODO Implement this method
        //Opción 1: La clase TrianguloRectangulo{} implementa su propio
        //   algoritmo del cálculo del área

        return (super.getAltura() * super.getBase()) / 2;

        //Opción 2: La clase TrianguloRectangulo{} invoca
        //   al algoritmo de calcular el área de la superclase Figura
        //return super.area();

    }

}
```

Explanation of the most relevant lines of code, pertaining to configuration 3.1 - variant 1

```java
package app;

import patron.Figura;
import patron.Rectangulo;
import patron.TrianguloRectangulo;

public class Main {
```

Declaration of the reference called figura. This reference is created using the superclass called Figura{} and will point to an object instance created by the subclass: Rectangulo{} or TrianguloRectangulo{}.

```java
    private static Figura figura = null;
```

```java
    public Main() {
        super();
    }
```

```
public static void main(String[] args) {

    Main main = new Main();

    System.out.println("Polimorfismo    dinámico,    una    referencia    muchos
objetos, con recolector de basura");
```

The next line of code will create a new object using the constructor named `Rectangulo()`.

```
figura = new Rectangulo(3, 4);
```

The following code will execute the polymorphic method called `polimorfismo(¿...?)`. The parameter of the method is of the figure type. And the argument is of the rectangle type. The assignment of the type in the argument at runtime is known as dynamic polymorphism.

```
polimorfismo(figura);
```

The reference called figure is pointed to a new object. The new object is created by the constructor called `TrianguloRectangulo()`. The object of type rectangle no longer has a valid referencing. The garbage collector of the JVM should clean the non-referenced objects.

```
figura = new TrianguloRectangulo(5, 4);
```

The following code will execute the polymorphic method called `polimorfismo(¿...?)`. The parameter of the method is of the figure type. And the argument is of the type of triangles that are rectangles. The assignment of the type in the argument at runtime is known as dynamic polymorphism. Any line of Java code that uses a polymorphic reference will be, by extension, a polymorphic code.

```
polimorfismo(figura);

}
```

The following code is the declaration of the polymorphic method called `polimorfismo()`, the dynamic polymorphic methods are characterized by having parameters of one type and the arguments of another type. The parameter is of the figure type and the arguments can be of the rectangle type and the triangle-rectangle type. Dynamic polymorphic methods have polymorphic algorithms; polymorphic algorithms are characterized by invoking different behaviors depending on the argument of the parameter. Dynamic polymorphic methods send messages to classes that have the role of behavior providers. The classes that have the role of clients implement polymorphic algorithms and the classes that have the role of providers implement specialized behavior algorithms. The main characteristic of dynamic polymorphic algorithms is that their behavior and the sending of messages are defined at runtime.

```
//Método polimórfico o sobrecargado por el argumento del parámetro
//El parámetro acepta tipos de argumentos distintos
//En algunas ocasiones el argumento es del tipo rectángulo
//  y en otras es del tipo triángulo rectángulo
private static void polimorfismo(Figura figura) {

    //Líneas polimórficas, tienen comportamiento distinto dependiendo de la
figura
    //El compilador Java decide que comportamiento ejecutar dependiendo del
tipo de argumento
```

```
        System.out.println(figura.getClass().getName());

        if(figura.area()>10)
          System.out.println(" Color = " + figura.getColor());

        System.out.println(" Altura = " + figura.getAltura());
        System.out.println(" Base = " + figura.getBase());
        System.out.println(" Área = " + figura.area());

    }
```

The following code is correct and demonstrates that it is feasible to overload the parameter of the method called `polimorfismo()` with two different types of arguments.

```
    private static void polimorfismo(Rectangulo figura) {
        //acceder a los métodos de Rectangulo{}, si es necesario

    }
    private static void polimorfismo(TrianguloRectangulo figura) {
        //acceder a los métodos de TrianguloRectangulo{}, si es necesario

    }
}//Fin del cuerpo de la clase Main{}
```

Important notes:

Polymorphic methods and polymorphic algorithms should be implemented in classes that are clients of a design pattern.

The specialized algorithms should be implemented in the design pattern, the design pattern is built by the classes that are related through inheritance.

Classes that have the role of clients benefit from implementing algorithms based on sending messages, reducing their code and reusing lines of code.

The design pattern will decide which specialized algorithm will execute depending on the parameters and arguments of the received message.

```
package patron;
```

```
import java.awt.Color;
```

The following code is the declaration of the superclass named `Figura{}`, the superclass will implement an interface named `CalcularArea{}`.

```
public class Figura implements CalcularArea {
```

```
    private Integer altura = 0;
    private Integer base = 0;
    private Color color = null;
```

The following methods are the public interface to access the private fields of the `Figura{}` class.

```
public Figura(Integer b, Integer a) {
    base = b; altura = a;
    //super();
}
public void setAltura(Integer altura) {
    this.altura = altura;
}

public void setBase(Integer base) {
    this.base = base;
}

public Integer getAltura() {
    return altura;
}

public Integer getBase() {
    return base;
}

public void setColor(Color color) {
    this.color = color;
}

public Color getColor() {
    return color;
}
```

The following code is the declaration that overwrites the abstract method called area(), the abstract method was declared in the interface named CalcularArea{}, the overriding method can implement the specialized algorithms for each subclass. If the subclasses are many, the superclass named Figura{} can give up writing specialized Java code and allow each subclass to implement its own algorithms. Normally subclasses are responsible for overwriting methods that are abstract and implement algorithms with a greater level of detail.

The programmers can decide to write the specialized algorithms in the subclasses or in the superclass, it is recommended to write the specialized code in the subclasses.

To execute Java code implemented in a superclass, subclasses can use the following Java keywords: super and this.

To execute Java code implemented in a subclass or in a superclass, the classes that have the client role will use the following options:
- Analysis of the type of object by the JVM, in execution time. (dynamic polymorphism)
- Analysis of the type of object by the JDK, at design time. (static polymorphism)

```
@Override
public Integer area() {

if(this.getClass().getName().equalsIgnoreCase(Rectangulo.class.getName())) {
        return altura * base;
    }else{
        return (altura * base) / 2;
    }
```

```
    }//fin del método abstracto sobrescrito

}//fin de la declaración de la clase Figura{}
```

The following code is the declaration of the subclass named `Rectangulo{}`. The subclass has inherited members of the superclass named `Figura{}`.

The subclass overwrites the abstract method, for the second time, called `area()`. The abstract method was implemented in the superclass `Figura{}`, the class `Rectangulo{}` has the opportunity to implement its own algorithm or invoke the algorithm already implemented in the class `Figura{}`.

```
package patron;

import java.awt.Color;

public class Rectangulo extends Figura {

    public Rectangulo(Integer b, Integer a) {

        super(b, a);//invocar el constructor de la clase Figura{}
        super.setColor(new  Color(Color.orange.getRGB()));//invocar  el  método
setColor() de la clase Figura{}

    }

    /////////////////////////
    //sobrescribir todos los métodos de la clase Figura{}, si es necesario
    /////////////////////////

    @Override
    public Color getColor() {
        // TODO Implement this method
        return super.getColor();
    }

    @Override
    public Integer area() {

        // TODO Implement this method
        //Opción 1: La clase Rectangulo{} implementa su propio
        //   algoritmo del cálculo del área

        //return super.getAltura() * super.getBase();

        //Opción 2: La clase Rectangulo{} invoca
        //   el algoritmo del cálculo del área de la superclase Figura{}
        return super.area();

    }

}
```

La clase `TrianguloRectangulo{}` sobrescribe el método `area()` implementado en la clase `Figura{}`, la clase `TrianguloRectangulo{}` tiene la oportunidad de implementar su propio algoritmo o invocar al algoritmo ya implementado en la clase `Figura{}`.

Los programadores pueden decidir escribir algoritmos especializados en las subclases o en la superclase, depende de las decisiones de los programadores o del problema que se quiera resolver.

The following code is the declaration of the subclass named `TrianguloRectangulo{}`. The subclass has inherited members of the superclass named `Figura{}`.

The subclass overwrites the abstract method, for the second time, called `area()`. The abstract method was implemented in the superclass `Figura{}`, the class `TrianguloRectangulo{}` has the opportunity to implement its own algorithm or invoke the algorithm already implemented in the class `Figura{}`.

```java
package patron;

import java.awt.Color;

public class TrianguloRectangulo extends Figura {
    public TrianguloRectangulo(Integer b, Integer a) {
        super(b, a); //invocar el constructor de la clase Figura{}
        super.setColor(new  Color(Color.green.getRGB()));//invocar  el   método
    setColor() de la clase Figura{}
    }

    ////////////////////////////
    //sobrescribir todos los métodos de la clase Figura{}, si es necesario
    ////////////////////////////

    @Override
    public Color getColor() {
        // TODO Implement this method
        return super.getColor();
    }

    @Override
    public Integer area() {

        // TODO Implement this method
        //Opción 1: La clase TrianguloRectangulo{} implementa su propio
        //  algoritmo del cálculo del área

        return (super.getAltura() * super.getBase()) / 2;

        //Opción 2: La clase TrianguloRectangulo{} invoca
        //  al algoritmo de calcular el área de la superclase Figura{}
        //return super.area();
    }
}
```

The following lines of code are the declaration of the interface with the name of `CalcularArea{}`, that interface will declare the prototypes of abstract methods. The following statement: `public Integer area();` it is the declaration of a prototype of an abstract method. Methods that are abstract have no body to implement Java code.

```
package patron;

public interface CalcularArea {

//agregar todas las obligaciones de implementación para la clase Figura{}

    public Integer area(); //método abstracto

}
```

The class that has the superclass role in the inheritance hierarchy is obliged to implement the abstract method called `area()`. The interface `CalcularArea{}` is a contract that the superclass `Figura{}` has to fulfill.

The contract declared by the `CalcularArea{}` interface could have more obligations for the superclass named `Figura{}`. For example:

```
package patron;

public interface CalcularArea {

    //agregar todas las obligaciones de implementación para la clase Figura{}

    public Integer area(); //método abstracto

    public void setColor(Color color); //nuevo contrato

    public Color getColor(); //nuevo contrato

}
```

Note: In the declaration of the interfaces, it is normally omitted: the use of the `static` access modifier and the `abstract` keyword.

The following code does not omit the use of keywords: `static` and `abstract`.

```
public abstract interface circulo {
    //superficie = pi * radio^2      //módulo de cálculo
    //perimetro = 2 * pi * radio     //módulo de cálculo
    public static float pi = 3.14f;  //campo constante y global
    public static float pi2 = 6.28f; //campo constante y global
    public   abstract   float   superficieCirculo(int   radio);   //método
    abstracto
    public   abstract   float   perimetroCirculo(int   radio);   //método
    abstracto
}
```

UML diagram in Java for configuration 3.1 - variant 2: many references and one object by reference

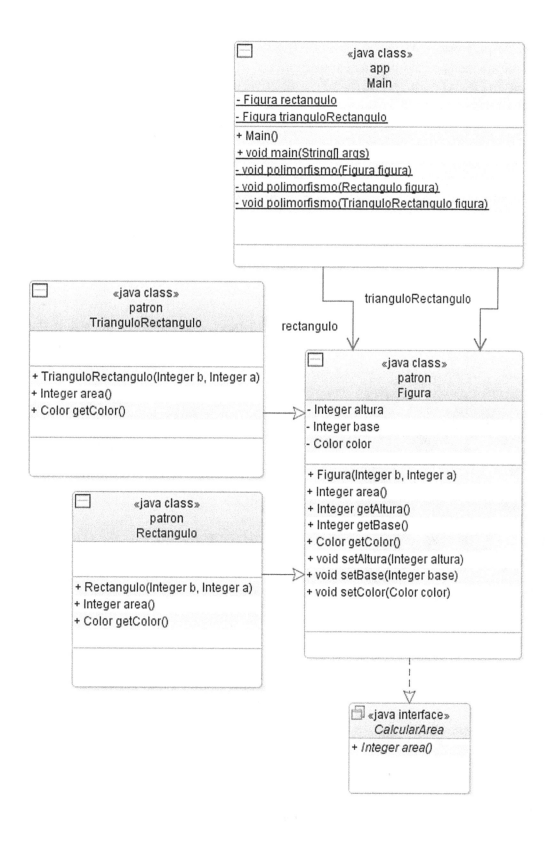

Characteristics of the configuration 3.1 - variant 2: many references and one object by reference

In the configuration 3.1 variant 2 two references are created using the superclass `Figura{}`, these references have the name of `rectangulo` and `trianguloRectangulo`. The references are pointed, respectively, to two instances of objects. These objects are instantiated using the constructor methods of the subclasses: `Rectangulo{}` and `TrianguloRectangulo{}`

The task or strategy of variant 2, is to create all references and objects at the start of the application and let them remain in memory for the entire duration of the execution of the application.

Variant 2 allows you to reduce the creation of objects at runtime. In this technique the use of the microprocessor is reduced but the amount of memory used increases. The JVM garbage collector has little work, since there are no objects not referenced at runtime.

Programmers must decide between variant 1 or variant 2, depending on the requirements of the system and the problem to be solved.

Source code for configuration 3.1 - variant 2

The following lines of code belong to the layer that has the client role, since it is the layer that underwent the modifications of variant 2. The rest of the source code is identical to variant 1.

```
package app;

import patron.Figura;
import patron.Rectangulo;
import patron.TrianguloRectangulo;

public class Main {
```

Declaration of the necessary references for configuration 3.1 variant 2

```
    private static Figura rectangulo = null;
    private static Figura trianguloRectangulo = null;

    public Main() {
        super();
    }

    public static void main(String[] args) {
        Main main = new Main();
        System.out.println("Pilimorfismo dinámico, una referencia por objeto,
sin recolector basura");
```

The next line of code creates a new object in memory using the constructor called `Rectangulo()`, that object will be pointed by the reference called `rectangulo`.

```
        rectangulo = new Rectangulo(3, 4);
```

The following code executes the polymorphic method called `polimorfismo()`, with the argument of type rectangle.

```
    polimorfismo(rectangulo);
```

The next line of code creates a new object in memory using the constructor called `TrianguloRectangulo()`, that object will be pointed by the reference called `trianguloRectangulo`.

```
    trianguloRectangulo = new TrianguloRectangulo(5, 4);
```

The following code executes the polymorphic method called `polimorfismo()`, with the argument of the type of triangles that are rectangles.

```
    polimorfismo(trianguloRectangulo);
}
```

The following lines of code are the declaration of the dynamic polymorphic method called `polimorfismo()`, dynamic polymorphic methods are characterized by having parameters of one type and arguments of another type. The parameter represents the figures in a generic way. The arguments of the parameter can be of the particular type: rectangle and triangle-rectangle. Polymorphic methods that are dynamic have polymorphic algorithms that are also dynamic; polymorphic algorithms that are dynamic are characterized by invoking different behaviors depending on the argument of the parameter. Polymorphic methods that are dynamic send messages to classes that have the role of providers. The classes that have the role of clients implement algorithms that are polymorphic and the classes that have the role of providers implement behavioral algorithms that are specialized. The main characteristic of algorithms that are polymorphic is that their behavior and the sending of messages are defined at runtime.

```
    //Método polimórfico o sobrecargado por el argumento del parámetro
    //El parámetro acepta tipos de argumentos distintos
    //En algunas ocasiones el argumento es del tipo rectángulo
    //  y en otras es del tipo triángulo rectángulo
    private static void polimorfismo(Figura figura) {
        //Líneas polimórficas, tienen comportamiento distinto dependiendo de la
figura
        //El compilador Java decide que comportamiento ejecutar dependiendo del
tipo de argumento
        System.out.println(figura.getClass().getName());
        if(figura.area()>10)
          System.out.println("  Color = " + figura.getColor());
        System.out.println("  Altura = " + figura.getAltura());
        System.out.println("  Base = " + figura.getBase());
        System.out.println("  Área = " + figura.area());


    }
```

The following code is correct and demonstrates that it is feasible to overload the parameter of the `polimorfismo()` method with two different types of arguments.

```
//    private static void polimorfismo(Rectangulo figura) {
//        //acceder a los métodos de la clase Rectangulo{}, si es necesario
//
//    }
//    private static void polimorfismo(TrianguloRectangulo figura) {
```

```
//           //acceder a los métodos de la clase TrianguloRectangulo{}, si es
   necesario
//
//     }

}//Fin del cuerpo de la clase Main{}
```

Important note:
Methods and algorithms that are polymorphic must be implemented in the classes that are clients of the design pattern; the design pattern is a hierarchy of related classes through inheritance. Algorithms that are specialized must be implemented in the design pattern. The programmers will make responsible the subclasses or the superclass of the implementation of the specialized algorithms. Classes that have the role of clients benefit from implementing the algorithms based on sending messages by reducing their code and reusing it. The design pattern must decide which algorithm to execute depending on the parameters and the arguments of the message that has been received.

Configuration 3.2 - Create references to objects and objects using subclasses

In configuration 3.2, two constraints are introduced that force the architecture to work properly and also force a good use of the design pattern based on the inheritance between classes.

Properties of configuration 3.2

	Create references	**Create objects**
Superclass (Interface)	X(Restriction)	X(Restriction)
Subclass	Yes	Yes

Configuration utility 3.2
It is a suitable configuration for when there are few specialized objects; each object has the need to implement a particular or unique algorithm. If as many references are created as specialized objects, then it is feasible to have an object in memory for each reference. Each reference works as a pointer to each specialized object. Objects can remain in memory during the entire execution time of the application without the need to collect non-referenced objects. This type of configuration allows the implementation of dynamic algorithms and static algorithms.

How to implement the algorithms that are static?
The implementation of the static algorithms is done by declaring a static method. Static methods have the parameter and the argument of the same type.

How to implement algorithms that are dynamic?
The implementation of the dynamic algorithms is done declaring a dynamic method. Dynamic methods have the parameter and the argument of different types.

What is the static assignment of the reference?
It is when a reference is assigned to an object during the entire execution of the application. In this type of assignment the JVM does not have much work since there are no objects not referenced in the memory.

What is the dynamic assignment of the reference?

It is when a reference is assigned to more than one object during the entire execution of the application. In this type of assignment, the JVM has a lot of work since it must clean objects not referenced in the memory.

To use the mechanism of polymorphism, messages are sent to objects through an interface with public methods. Each object must implement the same methods interface.

Configuration 3.2 has two variants:
1. in variant 1: the interface is implemented by the superclass
2. in variant 2: the interface is implemented by the subclass

Class diagram in Java for configuration 3.2 - variant 1

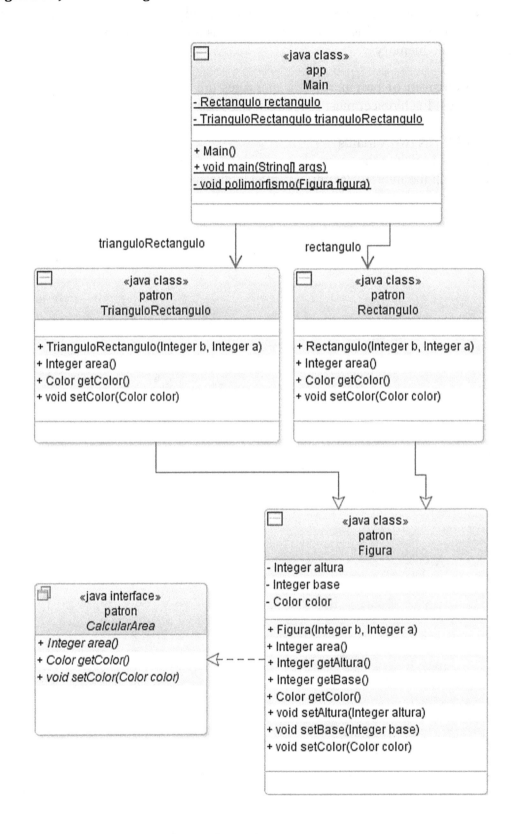

Source code for configuration 3.2 - variant 1

```java
package app;

import java.awt.Color;
import patron.Figura;
import patron.Rectangulo;
import patron.TrianguloRectangulo;

public class Main {
    public Main() {
        super();
    }

    private static Rectangulo rectangulo  = null;
    private static TrianguloRectangulo trianguloRectangulo = null;

    public static void main(String[] args) {

        Main main = new Main();

        System.out.println("Polimorfismo estático o dinámico.");
        rectangulo = new Rectangulo(3, 4);
        Color color = new Color(Color.blue.getRGB());
        rectangulo.setColor(color);
        polimorfismo(rectangulo);
        //System.out.println("Área rectángulo " + rectangulo.area());
        trianguloRectangulo = new TrianguloRectangulo(5, 4);
        color = new Color(Color.orange.getRGB());
        trianguloRectangulo.setColor(color);
        polimorfismo(trianguloRectangulo);
        //System.out.println("Área          triángulo          rectángulo          "          +
trianguloRectangulo.area());


    }

    //El método polimorfismo() puede ser sobrecargado de tres formas distintas
    //Este es un método polimórfico dinámico, un método polimórfico dinámico
tiene el parámetro de un tipo y los argumentos de otro tipo

    private static void polimorfismo(Figura figura) {

        //Algoritmo polimórfico dinámico, estas líneas de código se ejecutan de
igual forma para dos tipos distintos.
        //Las líneas de código polimórficas dinámicas tienen comportamiento
        //  distintos dependiendo del tipo de argumento.
        System.out.print(figura.getClass().getName());
        System.out.println("  Área = " + figura.area());
        System.out.println("  Color =  " + figura.getColor());
    }

    //Cuidado! si  las  siguientes  líneas  son  descomentadas  funcionaran
correctamente pero habría que comentar el método sobrecargado con el parámetro
del tipo Figura{}
    //Estas líneas de código demuestran que el parámetro y el argumento
    //  pueden ser de dos tipos diferentes
    //El programador decide en qué método sobrecargado quiere escribir código
    /*
```

```java
    //Este es un método polimórfico estático, un método polimórfico estático
tiene el parámetro y el argumento del mismo tipo.

    private static void polimorfismo(Rectangulo figura) {
        //acceder a los métodos de la clase Rectangulo{}, si es necesario

    }

    //Este es un método polimórfico estático, un método polimórfico estático
tiene el parámetro y el argumento del mismo tipo.
    private static void polimorfismo(TrianguloRectangulo figura) {
        //acceder a los métodos de clase Triangulo{}, si es necesario

    }
    */
}

package patron;

import java.awt.Color;

public class Figura implements CalcularArea {
    private Integer altura = 0;
    private Integer base = 0;
    private Color color = null;
    public Figura(Integer b, Integer a) {
        base = b; altura = a;
        //super();
    }
    public void setAltura(Integer altura) {
        this.altura = altura;
    }

    public void setBase(Integer base) {
        this.base = base;
    }

    public Integer getAltura() {
        return altura;
    }

    public Integer getBase() {
        return base;
    }

    @Override
    public Integer area() {
        //Los programadores han decidido que el cálculo de área
        //  quede a cargo de la superclase

if(this.getClass().getName().equalsIgnoreCase(Rectangulo.class.getName())) {
            return altura * base;
        }else{
            return (altura * base) / 2;
        }
    }

    @Override
    public Color getColor() {
```

```java
        // TODO Implement this method
        return color;
    }

    @Override
    public void setColor(Color color) {
        // TODO Implement this method
        this.color = color;
    }
}

package patron;

import java.awt.Color;

public class Rectangulo extends Figura {
    public Rectangulo(Integer b, Integer a) {
        super(b, a);
    }

    //Sobrescribir los métodos de la clase Figura{}
    @Override
    public Integer area() {

        // TODO Implement this method
        //return super.getAltura() * super.getBase();
        return super.area(); //el cálculo del área quedará a cargo de la
superclase

    }

    @Override
    public Color getColor() {
        // TODO Implement this method
        return super.getColor();
    }

    @Override
    public void setColor(Color color) {
        // TODO Implement this method
        super.setColor(color);
    }
}

package patron;

import java.awt.Color;

public class Rectangulo extends Figura {
    public Rectangulo(Integer b, Integer a) {
        super(b, a);
    }

    //Sobrescribir los métodos de la clase Figura{}
    @Override
    public Integer area() {

        // TODO Implement this method
        //return super.getAltura() * super.getBase();
```

```java
            return super.area(); //el cálculo del área quedará a cargo de la
superclase

    }

    @Override
    public Color getColor() {
        // TODO Implement this method
        return super.getColor();
    }

    @Override
    public void setColor(Color color) {
        // TODO Implement this method
        super.setColor(color);
    }
}

package patron;

import java.awt.Color;

public interface CalcularArea {

    public Integer area();
    public Color getColor();
    public void setColor(Color color);

}
```

Class diagram in Java for configuration 3.2 - variant 2

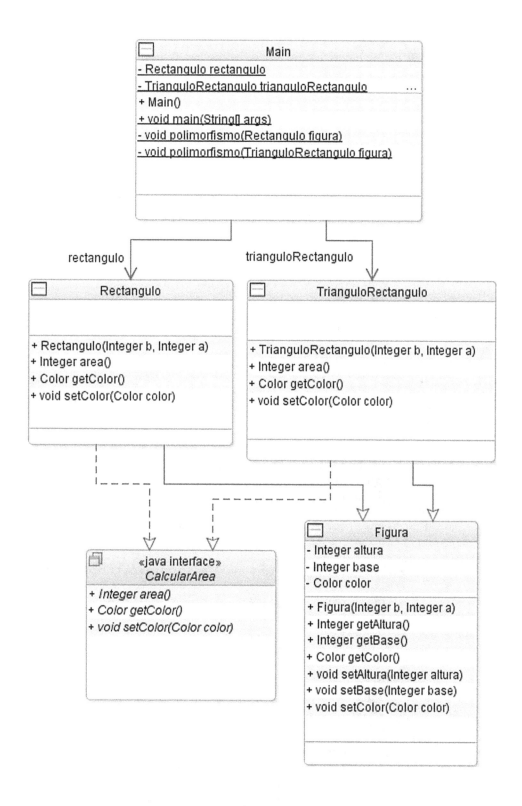

Source code for configuration 3.2 - variant 2

```java
package app;

import java.awt.Color;

import patron.Figura;
import patron.Rectangulo;
import patron.TrianguloRectangulo;

public class Main {
    public Main() {
        super();
    }
    private static Rectangulo rectangulo  = null;
    private static TrianguloRectangulo trianguloRectangulo = null;
    public static void main(String[] args) {
        Main main = new Main();
        System.out.println("Polimorfismo estático o dinámico");
        Color color = new Color(Color.blue.getRGB());
        rectangulo = new Rectangulo(3, 4);
        rectangulo.setColor(color);
        polimorfismo(rectangulo);
        //System.out.println("Área rectángulo " + rectangulo.area());
        color = new Color(Color.orange.getRGB());
        trianguloRectangulo = new TrianguloRectangulo(5, 4);
        trianguloRectangulo.setColor(color);
        polimorfismo(trianguloRectangulo);
        //System.out.println("Área        triángulo        rectángulo        "        +
trianguloRectangulo.area());
    }
    //Método polimórfico estático, un método polimórfico estático tiene el
    //parámetro y el argumento del mismo tipo.
    private static void polimorfismo(Rectangulo figura) {
        //Algoritmo polimórfico estático
        System.out.print(figura.getClass().getName());
        System.out.println(" Área = " + figura.area());
        if(figura.area()>10)
            System.out.println(" Color =  " + figura.getColor());
    }
    //Método polimórfico estático, un método polimórfico estático tiene el
    //parámetro y el argumento del mismo tipo.
    private static void polimorfismo(TrianguloRectangulo figura) {
        //Algoritmo polimórfico estático
        System.out.print(figura.getClass().getName());
        System.out.println(" Área = " + figura.area());
        if(figura.area()>10)
            System.out.println(" Color =  " + figura.getColor());
    }
    //!Cuidado¡ Este método polimórfico dinámico se ha comentado.
    //Este método si es descomentado funcionará perfectamente pero si
    //   es descomentado es preferible usarlo con una referencia del tipo
Figura{} y objetos creados con las subclases.
/*    private static void polimorfismo(Figura figura) {
        //acceder a los métodos de Figura{}, si es necesario.
        //Escribir un algoritmo polimórfico dinámico


    }
*/
```

```
}

package patron;

import java.awt.Color;

public class Figura {
    private Integer altura = 0;
    private Integer base = 0;
    private Color color = null;

    public void setColor(Color color) {
        this.color = color;
    }

    public Color getColor() {
        return color;
    }

    public Figura(Integer b, Integer a) {
        base = b; altura = a;
        //super();
    }
    public void setAltura(Integer altura) {
        this.altura = altura;
    }

    public void setBase(Integer base) {
        this.base = base;
    }

    public Integer getAltura() {
        return altura;
    }

    public Integer getBase() {
        return base;
    }
}

package patron;

import java.awt.Color;

public class Rectangulo extends Figura implements CalcularArea {
    public Rectangulo(Integer b, Integer a) {
        super(b, a);
    }
    //Sobrescribir los métodos de la clase Figura{}
    @Override
    public Integer area() {
        return this.getAltura() * this.getBase();
    }

    @Override
    public void setColor(Color color) {
        // TODO Implement this method
        super.setColor(color);
    }
```

```java
    @Override
    public Color getColor() {
        // TODO Implement this method
        return super.getColor();
    }
}


package patron;

import java.awt.Color;

public class TrianguloRectangulo extends Figura implements CalcularArea {
    public TrianguloRectangulo(Integer b, Integer a) {
        super(b, a);
    }
    //Sobrescribir los métodos de la clase Figura{}
    @Override
    public Integer area() {
        return (this.getAltura() * this.getBase()) / 2;
    }


    @Override
    public Color getColor() {
        // TODO Implement this method
        return super.getColor();
    }

    @Override
    public void setColor(Color color) {
        // TODO Implement this method
        super.setColor(color);
    }
}

package patron;

import java.awt.Color;

public interface CalcularArea {

    public Integer area();
    public Color getColor();
    public void setColor(Color color);

}
```

Chapter III

Polymorphic algorithms that are mutable

To create mutable polymorphic algorithms, it is necessary to declare references to objects with special classes of the interface type.

What are mutable polymorphic algorithms?

Given a hierarchy of inheritances between classes, it is feasible to create mutable polymorphic algorithms. These algorithms use references that have the property of being referenced to objects created with superclasses or subclasses.

What are mutable methods?

It is the ability of the methods to have parameters declared with an interface and the arguments of the parameters created with subclasses or superclasses.

An interface is an abstract class where all its methods are abstract and all its fields are constant. The interfaces do not implement the source code; the code must be implemented by the classes that inherit the interface. The interfaces are inherited using the Java keyword: `implements`.

There are different combinations with respect to the classes that can implement the interface.

Combination number 1:
- The interface is implemented by the superclass
  - The references are declared with the interfaces
  - Objects are created by the superclass or subclasses

Properties of the configuration for the combination 1

	Create references	Create objects
Superclass	-	Yes
Subclass	-	Yes
Interface	Yes	X(Can not)

The combination number 1, allows the mutability of the reference between the created objects with the subclasses and the superclass.

Combination number 2:
- The interface is implemented by subclasses
  - The references are declared with the interfaces
  - Objects are created with subclasses

Configuration properties for combination 2

	Create references	Create objects
Superclass	-	X(Can not)
Subclass	-	Yes
Interface	Yes	X(Can not)

The combination number 2, does not allow the mutability of the reference between the objects created with the subclasses and the superclass. The combination number 2 only allows you to create objects with subclasses.

Despite the impossibility of not creating objects from the superclass, it is still possible to create dynamic polymorphic algorithms using the combination number 2. Dynamic polymorphic algorithms were studied in chapters I and II.

For combinations numbers 1 and 2 there are two variants:
1. Declaring: a reference and many objects. (The reference must be reassigned to each of the objects during the execution of the application.) The JVM has a lot of work collecting non-referenced objects during the execution of the application.)
2. Declaring: many references, a reference for each object in memory. (The JVM usually has less work since it does not have to collect objects not referenced in memory)

Next, the class diagrams for variant number 1 of the combinations numbers 1 and 2 will be presented. The reader should make an effort and try to implement variant number 2.

The source code will not be commented, as there would be no new contributions to the comments made previously.

Class diagram for polymorphic algorithms that are mutable. Combination 1 - variant 1

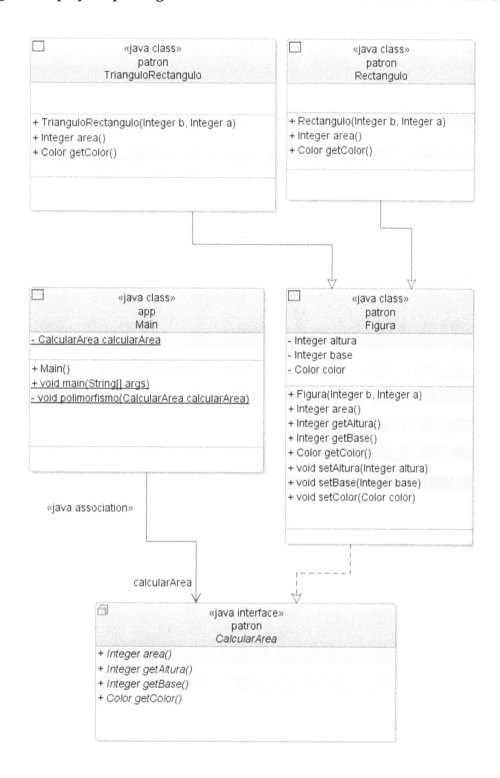

Source code that implements mutable polymorphic algorithms. Combination 1 - variant 1

```java
package app;

import patron.CalcularArea;
import patron.Figura;
import patron.Rectangulo;
import patron.TrianguloRectangulo;

public class Main {
    //Referencia del tipo Interfaz, esta referencia podrá mutar de ser
    una subclase a una superclase.
    private static CalcularArea calcularArea = null;

    public Main() {
        super();
    }

    public static void main(String[] args) {
        Main main = new Main();

        System.out.println("Polimorfismo mutable dinámico. Una referencia
        muchos objetos, con recolector de basura");

        calcularArea = new Figura(3, 4); //Mutación de la referencia al
        tipo superclase Figura{}
        polimorfismo(calcularArea);

        calcularArea = new Rectangulo(3, 4); //Mutación de la referencia
        al tipo subclase Rectangulo{}.
        polimorfismo(calcularArea);

        calcularArea = new TrianguloRectangulo(5, 4); //Mutación de la
        referencia al tipo subclase TrianguloRectangulo{}.
        polimorfismo(calcularArea);
    }
    //Método polimórfico o sobrecargado por el argumento del parámetro
    con mutación de superclase y subclases
    //El parámetro acepta tipos de argumentos distintos y de clases
    distintas en la jerarquía de herencia.
    //El parámetro es del tipo CalcularArea{}
    //Los argumentos pueden ser de los tipos: rectángulo, triángulo
    rectángulo definidos en las subclases.
    //También los argumentos pueden ser del tipo: figura, definidos en la
    superclase.
    private static void polimorfismo(CalcularArea calcularArea) {
        //Líneas polimórficas mutables, tienen comportamiento distinto
        dependiendo de los tipos de figuras en el argumento del parámetro y de
        las clases que construyen la jerarquía de herencia.
        //El compilador JDK, en tiempo de diseño, no tiene información de
        los tipos del argumento.
        //La JVM decide en tiempo de ejecución qué comportamiento
        ejecutar dependiendo de los tipos de argumentos.
        System.out.println(calcularArea.getClass().getName());
```

```
        System.out.println("  Altura = " + calcularArea.getAltura());
        System.out.println("  Base = " + calcularArea.getBase());
        System.out.println("  Área = " + calcularArea.area());
    }//Fin del método polimórfico dinámico mutable.

}//Fin del cuerpo de la clase Main{}.

package patron;

import java.awt.Color;

public interface CalcularArea {
    //Agregar todas las obligaciones de implementación para las clases
  que hereden esta Interfaz.
    public Color getColor();
    public Integer getBase();
    public Integer getAltura();
    public Integer area();
}

package patron;

import java.awt.Color;

public class Figura implements CalcularArea {
    private Integer altura = 0;
    private Integer base = 0;
    private Color color = null;

    public Figura(Integer b, Integer a) {
        base = b; altura = a;
        //super();
    }
    public void setAltura(Integer altura) {
        this.altura = altura;
    }

    public void setBase(Integer base) {
        this.base = base;
    }

    @Override
    public Integer getAltura() {
        return altura;
    }

    @Override
    public Integer getBase() {
        return base;
    }

    public void setColor(Color color) {
        this.color = color;
    }
```

```java
    @Override
    public Color getColor() {
        return color;
    }

    //En muchos problemas reales este método puede ser comentado o no
usado, se ha implementado por motivos didácticos, es preferible que las
subclases se dediquen a los aspectos concretos del problema a resolver.
    @Override
    public Integer area() {


if(this.getClass().getName().equalsIgnoreCase(Rectangulo.class.getName(
))) {
            return altura * base;
        }


if(this.getClass().getName().equalsIgnoreCase(TrianguloRectangulo.class
.getName())) {
            return (altura * base) / 2;
        }

        System.out.println("Esta mutación de la referencia no determina
el tipo de figura.");
        System.out.println("          Mutación      usada:      "      +
this.getClass().getName());
        System.out.println("        dicha mutación puede realizar tareas
generales y no particulares (abstractas y no concretas)");
        return 0;
    }//fin del método abstracto sobrescrito.
}//fin de la declaración de la clase Figura{}.

package patron;

import java.awt.Color;

public class Rectangulo extends Figura {
    public Rectangulo(Integer b, Integer a) {
        super(b, a);//invocar al constructor de la clase Figura{}
        super.setColor(new   Color(Color.orange.getRGB()));//invocar   al
método setColor() de la clase Figura{}
    }
    /////////////////////////
    //Sobrescribir todos los métodos de la clase Figura{}, si es
necesario.
    /////////////////////////

    @Override
    public Color getColor() {
        // TODO Implement this method
        return super.getColor();
    }
```

```java
    @Override
    public Integer area() {
        // TODO Implement this method
        //Opción 1 (recomendada): La clase Rectangulo{} implementa su
propio algoritmo del cálculo del área.
        return super.getAltura() * super.getBase();

        //Opción 2 (no recomendada): La clase Rectangulo{} invoca al
algoritmo del cálculo del área de la superclase Figura{}.
        //return super.area();
    }
}

package patron;

import java.awt.Color;

public class TrianguloRectangulo extends Figura {

    public TrianguloRectangulo(Integer b, Integer a) {
        super(b, a);
        super.setColor(new Color(Color.green.getRGB()));
    }
    ///////////////////////////
    //Sobrescribir todos los métodos de la clase Figura{}, si es
necesario.
    ///////////////////////////

    @Override
    public Color getColor() {
        // TODO Implement this method
        return super.getColor();
    }

    @Override
    public Integer area() {
        // TODO Implement this method
        //Opción 1 (recomendada): La clase TrianguloRectangulo{}
implementa su propio algoritmo del cálculo del área.
        return (super.getAltura() * super.getBase()) / 2;

        //Opción 2 (no recomendada): La clase TrianguloRectangulo{}
invoca al algoritmo de calcular el área de la superclase Figura{}.
        //return super.area();
    }
}
```

Class diagram in UML for mutable polymorphic algorithms. Combination 2 - variant 1

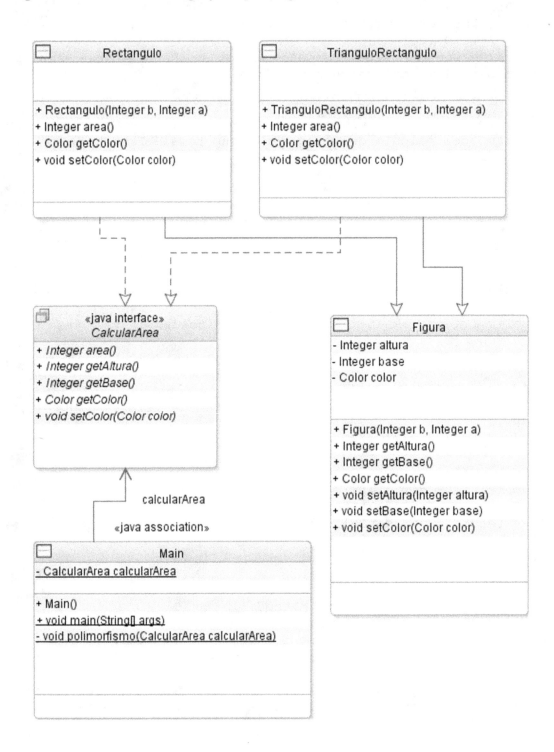

Source code that implements mutable polymorphic algorithms. Combination 2, variant 1

```java
package app;

import patron.CalcularArea;
import patron.Rectangulo;
import patron.TrianguloRectangulo;

public class Main {
    //Referencia del tipo Interfaz, esta referencia podrá mutar de ser
    una subclase a una superclase.
    private static CalcularArea calcularArea = null;
    public Main() {
        super();
    }

    public static void main(String[] args) {
        Main main = new Main();

        System.out.println("Polimorfismo dinámico no mutable entre clases
    de la jerarquía de herencia. Una referencia muchos objetos, con
    recolector de basura");

        //Lamentablemente la implementación de la interfaz CalcularArea{}
    por parte de las subclases no permite la mutabilidad a la superclase
    Figura{}.
        //calcularArea = new Figura(3, 4); //Mutación de la referencia al
    tipo superclase, Figura{}, no permitida.
        //polimorfismo(calcularArea); //No descomentar, dará error del
    compilador.

        calcularArea = new Rectangulo(3, 4); //Mutación de la referencia
    al tipo subclase Rectangulo{}.
        polimorfismo(calcularArea);

        calcularArea = new TrianguloRectangulo(5, 4); //Mutación de la
    referencia al tipo subclase TrianguloRectangulo{}.
        polimorfismo(calcularArea);
    }
    //Método polimórfico o sobrecargado por el argumento del parámetro
    sin mutación a la superclase.
    //El parámetro acepta tipos de argumentos distintos pertenecientes a
    las subclases.
    //El parámetro es del tipo CalcularArea{}. Los argumentos pueden ser
    de los tipos: rectángulo, triángulo rectángulo definidas en las
    subclases.
    //No está permitido que los argumentos pueden ser del tipo: figura,
    definida en la superclase.
    //Este es un método polimórfico dinámico pero no mutable entre las
    clases de la jerarquía de herencia.
    private static void polimorfismo(CalcularArea calcularArea) {
        //Líneas polimórficas dinámicas, tienen comportamiento distinto
    dependiendo de los tipos de figuras en el argumento del parámetro.
        //El compilador JDK, en tiempo de diseño, no tiene información de
```

```
        los tipos del argumento.
            //La  JVM  decide  en  tiempo  de  ejecución  qué  comportamiento
        ejecutar dependiendo de los tipos de argumentos.
            //Este es un algoritmo polimórfico dinámico pero no mutable entre
        las clases de la jerarquía de herencia.
            System.out.println(calcularArea.getClass().getName());
            System.out.println("  Altura = " + calcularArea.getAltura());
            System.out.println("  Base = " + calcularArea.getBase());
            System.out.println("  Área = " + calcularArea.area());
        }//Fin del método polimórfico dinámico mutable.

}//Fin del cuerpo de la clase Main{}.

package patron;

import java.awt.Color;

public interface CalcularArea {
    public Integer area();
    public Color getColor();
    public Integer getBase();
    public Integer getAltura();
    public void setColor(Color color);
}

package patron;

import java.awt.Color;

//La clase Figura{} se ha declarado sin modificador de acceso para
  ocultarla, encapsularla, y no permitir el acceso desde el paquete app.
class Figura {
    private Integer altura = 0;
    private Integer base = 0;
    private Color color = null;

    public void setColor(Color color) {
        this.color = color;
    }

    public Color getColor() {
        return color;
    }

    public Figura(Integer b, Integer a) {
        base = b; altura = a;
        //super();
    }
    public void setAltura(Integer altura) {
        this.altura = altura;
    }

    public void setBase(Integer base) {
        this.base = base;
```

```java
    }

    public Integer getAltura() {
        return altura;
    }

    public Integer getBase() {
        return base;
    }
}

package patron;

import java.awt.Color;

public class Rectangulo extends Figura implements CalcularArea {
    public Rectangulo(Integer b, Integer a) {
        super(b, a);
    }
    //Sobrescribir los métodos den la clase Figura{}
    @Override
    public Integer area() {
        return this.getAltura() * this.getBase();
    }

    @Override
    public void setColor(Color color) {
        // TODO Implement this method
        super.setColor(color);
    }

    @Override
    public Color getColor() {
        // TODO Implement this method
        return super.getColor();
    }
}

package patron;

import java.awt.Color;

public class TrianguloRectangulo extends Figura implements CalcularArea {
    public TrianguloRectangulo(Integer b, Integer a) {
        super(b, a);
    }

    //Sobrescribir los métodos den la clase Figura{}

    @Override
    public Integer area() {
        return (this.getAltura() * this.getBase()) / 2;
    }
```

```java
    @Override
    public Color getColor() {
        // TODO Implement this method
        return super.getColor();
    }

    @Override
    public void setColor(Color color) {
        // TODO Implement this method
        super.setColor(color);
    }
}
```

Chapter IV

Programming a computer game

The following lines of code are a classic, computer game that applies polymorphic algorithms to control the characters in the game. Each character in the game will implement the algorithms that specialize in their behavior.

Configuration 3.2, variant number 1 of chapter II, will be used to write the source code of the game "Fly to the end". It is proposed to the reader, as a challenge, to make the necessary changes in the source code of the game to rewrite them as a mutable polymorphic algorithm discussed in Chapter III.

In the class that has the role of client, a reference will be declared for each character in the game. Each of the references will point to an object instance that will represent a character in the game.

The class that has the client role will implement a dynamic polymorphic method whose parameter will be of a generic type. And the arguments will be of the types, particular, of each character of the game.

The parameter of the polymorphic method will have the highest level of abstraction and will represent all the characters of the game, and the arguments of the parameter will have the lowest level of abstraction representing each of the characters in the game.

Polymorphic code of the game

The following line of source code is polymorphic, the parameter is an object reference called g2DMiLienzo and the arguments of the parameter can be of the type: Fondo{}, Nubes{}, Personaje{} o Pilares{}

```
        that Object.pickPolimorphism (g2DMiLienzo);
```

The reference with the name of g2DMiLienzo is of the type: DatosJuego{}. And it will point to instances of type objects: Fondo{}, Nubes{}, Personaje{} o Pilares{}

This line of code will be executed whenever it is necessary to paint an element on the game board.

Classes that have the role of being customers of the software design pattern benefit from reusing the source code and simplifying the logic of the game.

Each time the line of polymorphic code is executed, the JVM will decide which specialized code it will execute depending on the type of reference to instances of objects.

View of the computer game: Fly to the end

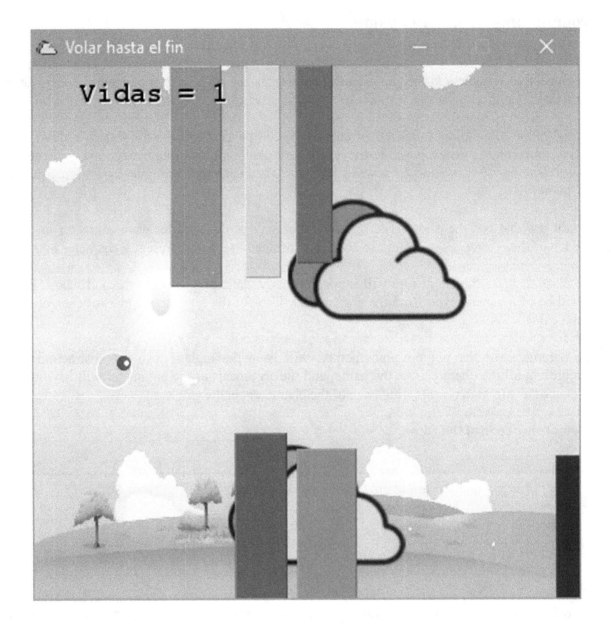

Class diagram in Java for the Game: Fly to the end

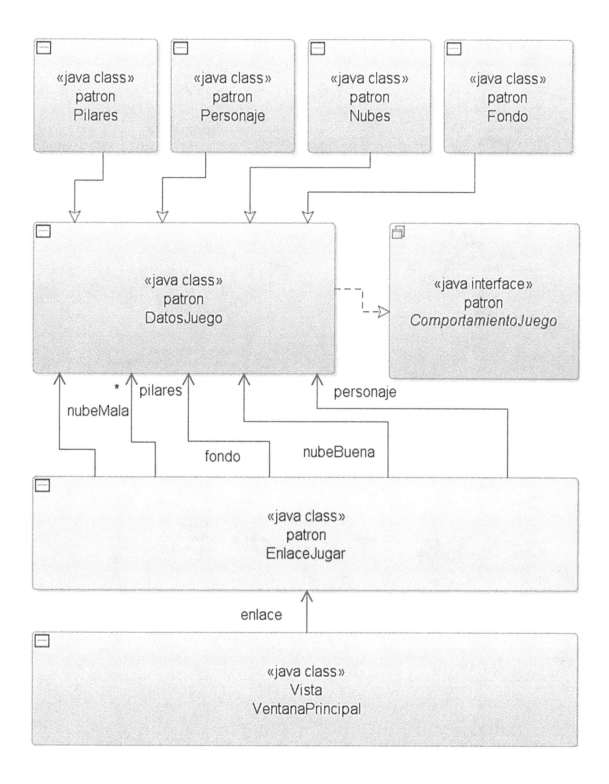

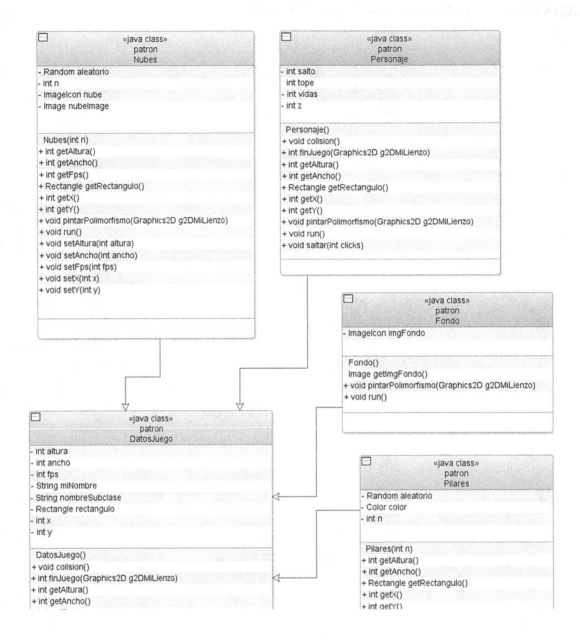

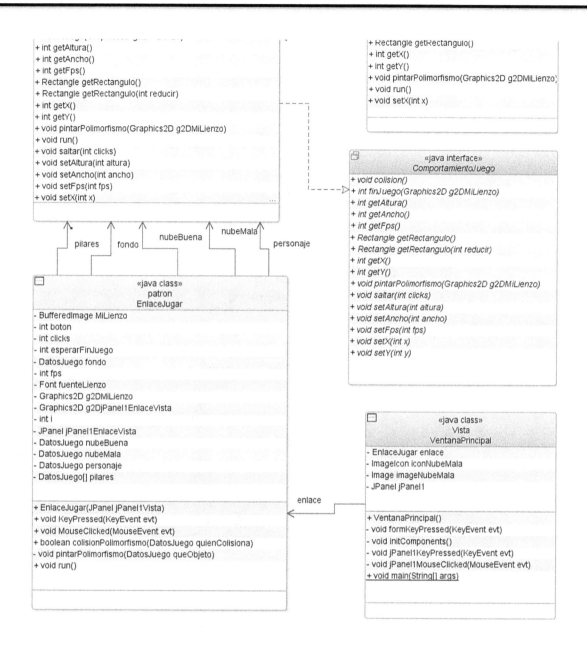

+ int getAltura()
+ int getAncho()
+ int getFps()
+ Rectangle getRectangulo()
+ Rectangle getRectangulo(int reducir)
+ int getX()
+ int getY()
+ void pintarPolimorfismo(Graphics2D g2DMiLienzo)
+ void run()
+ void saltar(int clicks)
+ void setAltura(int altura)
+ void setAncho(int ancho)
+ void setFps(int fps)
+ void setX(int x)

+ Rectangle getRectangulo()
+ int getX()
+ int getY()
+ void pintarPolimorfismo(Graphics2D g2DMiLienzo)
+ void run()
+ void setX(int x)

«java interface»
ComportamientoJuego

+ void colision()
+ int finJuego(Graphics2D g2DMiLienzo)
+ int getAltura()
+ int getAncho()
+ int getFps()
+ Rectangle getRectangulo()
+ Rectangle getRectangulo(int reducir)
+ int getX()
+ int getY()
+ void pintarPolimorfismo(Graphics2D g2DMiLienzo)
+ void saltar(int clicks)
+ void setAltura(int altura)
+ void setAncho(int ancho)
+ void setFps(int fps)
+ void setX(int x)
+ void setY(int y)

pilares   fondo   nubeBuena   nubeMala   personaje

«java class»
patron
EnlaceJugar

- BufferedImage MiLienzo
- int boton
- int clicks
- int esperarFinJuego
- DatosJuego fondo
- int fps
- Font fuenteLienzo
- Graphics2D g2DMiLienzo
- Graphics2D g2DjPanel1EnlaceVista
- int i
- JPanel jPanel1EnlaceVista
- DatosJuego nubeBuena
- DatosJuego nubeMala
- DatosJuego personaje
- DatosJuego[] pilares

+ EnlaceJugar(JPanel jPanel1Vista)
+ void KeyPressed(KeyEvent evt)
+ void MouseClicked(MouseEvent evt)
+ boolean colisionPolimorfismo(DatosJuego quienColisiona)
- void pintarPolimorfismo(DatosJuego queObjeto)
+ void run()

enlace

«java class»
Vista
VentanaPrincipal

- EnlaceJugar enlace
- ImageIcon iconNubeMala
- Image imageNubeMala
- JPanel jPanel1

+ VentanaPrincipal()
- void formKeyPressed(KeyEvent evt)
- void initComponents()
- void jPanel1KeyPressed(KeyEvent evt)
- void jPanel1MouseClicked(MouseEvent evt)
+ void main(String[] args)

Structure of folders and packages for the source code in Java

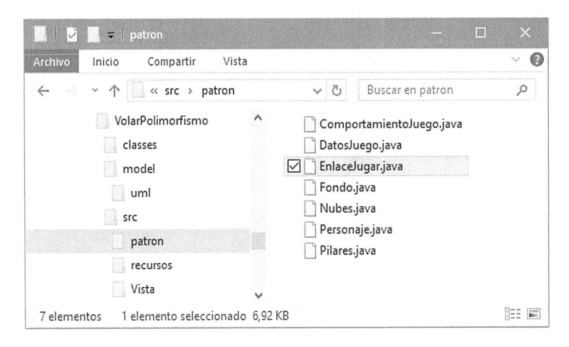

Source code in Java for the game view module

```java
package vista;
import java.awt.Graphics;
import java.awt.Image;
import javax.swing.ImageIcon;
import patron.EnlaceJugar;

public class VentanaPrincipal extends javax.swing.JFrame {
    private ImageIcon iconNubeMala = new
  ImageIcon(getClass().getResource("/recursos/nubeMala.png"));
    private Image imageNubeMala= null;
    private EnlaceJugar enlace = null;

    /** Creates new form VentanaPrincipal */
    public VentanaPrincipal() {
        imageNubeMala = iconNubeMala.getImage();
        initComponents();
        jPanel1.setIgnoreRepaint(false);
        enlace = new EnlaceJugar(this.jPanel1);
        enlace.start();
    }

    /** This method is called from within the constructor to
     * initialize the form.
     * WARNING: Do NOT modify this code. The content of this method is
     * always regenerated by the Form Editor.
     */
    @SuppressWarnings("unchecked")
    private void initComponents() {//GEN-BEGIN:initComponents

        jPanel1 = new javax.swing.JPanel(){
            @Override
            public void paint(Graphics graphics) {
                // TODO Implement this method
                super.paint(graphics);
                graphics.drawString("Cargando ...", 100, 100);
            }
            @Override
            public void update(Graphics graphics) {
                // TODO Implement this method
                super.update(graphics);
            }
        };

    setDefaultCloseOperation(javax.swing.WindowConstants.EXIT_ON_CLOSE);
```

```java
        setTitle("Volar hasta el fin");
        setIconImage(imageNubeMala);
        setMinimumSize(new java.awt.Dimension(400, 400));
        setResizable(false);
        addKeyListener(new java.awt.event.KeyAdapter() {
            public void keyPressed(java.awt.event.KeyEvent evt) {
                formKeyPressed(evt);
            }
        });

        jPanel1.setBackground(new java.awt.Color(204, 255, 204));
        jPanel1.addMouseListener(new java.awt.event.MouseAdapter() {
            public void mouseClicked(java.awt.event.MouseEvent evt) {
                jPanel1MouseClicked(evt);
            }
        });
        jPanel1.addKeyListener(new java.awt.event.KeyAdapter() {
            public void keyPressed(java.awt.event.KeyEvent evt) {
                jPanel1KeyPressed(evt);
            }
        });
        jPanel1.setLayout(null);
        getContentPane().add(jPanel1, java.awt.BorderLayout.CENTER);

        pack();
        setLocationRelativeTo(null);
    }//GEN-END:initComponents

    private void jPanel1MouseClicked(java.awt.event.MouseEvent evt)
    {//GEN-FIRST:event_jPanel1MouseClicked
        // TODO add your handling code here:
        enlace.MouseClicked(evt);
    }//GEN-LAST:event_jPanel1MouseClicked

    private void jPanel1KeyPressed(java.awt.event.KeyEvent evt) {//GEN-
    FIRST:event_jPanel1KeyPressed
        // TODO add your handling code here:
    }//GEN-LAST:event_jPanel1KeyPressed

    private void formKeyPressed(java.awt.event.KeyEvent evt) {//GEN-
    FIRST:event_formKeyPressed
        // TODO add your handling code here:
        enlace.KeyPressed(evt);
    }//GEN-LAST:event_formKeyPressed

    /**
     * @param args the command line arguments
```

```java
 */
public static void main(String args[]) {
    /* Set the Nimbus look and feel */
    //<editor-fold defaultstate="collapsed" desc=" Look and feel
setting code (optional) ">
    /* If Nimbus (introduced in Java SE 6) is not available, stay
with the default look and feel.
     * For details see
http://download.oracle.com/javase/tutorial/uiswing/lookandfeel/plaf.htm
l
     */
    try {
        for (javax.swing.UIManager.LookAndFeelInfo info : javax.swing

.UIManager

.getInstalledLookAndFeels()) {
            if ("Nimbus".equals(info.getName())) {
                javax.swing
                    .UIManager
                    .setLookAndFeel(info.getClassName());
                break;
            }
        }
    } catch (ClassNotFoundException ex) {
        java.util
            .logging
            .Logger
            .getLogger(VentanaPrincipal.class.getName())
            .log(java.util
                .logging
                .Level
                .SEVERE, null, ex);
    } catch (InstantiationException ex) {
        java.util
            .logging
            .Logger
            .getLogger(VentanaPrincipal.class.getName())
            .log(java.util
                .logging
                .Level
                .SEVERE, null, ex);
    } catch (IllegalAccessException ex) {
        java.util
            .logging
            .Logger
            .getLogger(VentanaPrincipal.class.getName())
```

```
                    .log(java.util
                            .logging
                            .Level
                            .SEVERE, null, ex);
        } catch (javax.swing.UnsupportedLookAndFeelException ex) {
            java.util
                    .logging
                    .Logger
                    .getLogger(VentanaPrincipal.class.getName())
                    .log(java.util
                            .logging
                            .Level
                            .SEVERE, null, ex);
        }
        //</editor-fold>

        /* Create and display the form */
        java.awt
            .EventQueue
            .invokeLater(new Runnable() {
                public void run() {
                    new VentanaPrincipal().setVisible(true);
                }
            });
    }

    // Variables declaration - do not modify//GEN-BEGIN:variables
    private javax.swing.JPanel jPanel1;
    // End of variables declaration//GEN-END:variables

}
```

Source code for the classes that implement the client module

```
package patron;

import java.awt.Font;
import java.awt.Graphics2D;
import java.awt.RenderingHints;
import java.awt.image.BufferedImage;
import javax.swing.JPanel;

//Esta clase es pública, las demás clases en el paquete son declaradas
sin el modificador de acceso

public class EnlaceJugar extends Thread {
    private int fps = 0, esperarFinJuego = 0, i = 0;
    private int boton = 0, clicks = 0;
```

```
    //Crear muchas referencias de un único tipo, DatosJuego{}

    private DatosJuego personaje = null;
    private DatosJuego[] pilares= new Pilares[8];
    private DatosJuego nubeBuena = null;
    private DatosJuego nubeMala = null;
    private DatosJuego fondo = null;

    private JPanel jPanel1EnlaceVista=null;
    private Graphics2D g2DjPanel1EnlaceVista = null;

    private BufferedImage miLienzo = null;
    private Graphics2D g2DMiLienzo = null;
    private Font fuenteLienzo = null;

    public EnlaceJugar(JPanel jPanel1Vista) {
        super();
        fps = 1000 / 70; esperarFinJuego = 0;

        //Creando un lienzo personalizado

        miLienzo = new BufferedImage(400,400,
BufferedImage.TYPE_INT_RGB);
        g2DMiLienzo = miLienzo.createGraphics();
        fuenteLienzo = new  Font("Courier", Font.BOLD, 20);
        g2DMiLienzo.setFont(fuenteLienzo);

        //Obtener el lienzo desde la vista

        jPanel1EnlaceVista = jPanel1Vista;
        g2DjPanel1EnlaceVista = (Graphics2D)
jPanel1EnlaceVista.getGraphics();

        //Full anti-alias
        g2DMiLienzo.setRenderingHint(RenderingHints.KEY_ANTIALIASING,
RenderingHints.VALUE_ANTIALIAS_ON);

        //Anti-alias para el texto

//g2DMiLienzo.setRenderingHint(RenderingHints.KEY_TEXT_ANTIALIASING,
RenderingHints.VALUE_TEXT_ANTIALIAS_ON);

        //Crear los objetos que deben ser pintados en el lienzo
personalizado

        fondo = new Fondo(); //Crear un objeto del tipo Fondo{} usando la
referencia del tipo DatosJuego{}

        fondo.start();//Lanzar un hilo personalizado para el objeto fondo

        personaje = new Personaje();//Crear un objeto del tipo
Personaje{} usando la referencia del tipo DatosJuego{}
```

```
        personaje.start();//Lanzar un hilo personalizado para el objeto
personaje

        for(int i=0; i<pilares.length;i++){

            pilares[i] = new Pilares(i);//Crear un objeto del tipo
Pilares{} usando la referencia del tipo DatosJuego{}

            pilares[i].start();//Lanzar un hilo personalizado para el
objeto pilar

        }
        nubeBuena = new Nubes(1);//Crear un objeto del tipo Nubes{}
usando la referencia del tipo DatosJuego{}

        nubeBuena.start();//Lanzar un hilo personalizado para el objeto
nube

        nubeMala = new Nubes(2);//Crear un objeto del tipo Nubes{} usando
la referencia del tipo DatosJuego{}

        nubeMala.start();//Lanzar un hilo personalizado para el objeto
nube

    }

    @Override
    public void run() {
        // TODO Implement this method
        super.run();
        do {
            try {
                //pintar el fondo
                pintarPolimorfismo(fondo);
                //pintar las nubes
                pintarPolimorfismo(nubeBuena);
                pintarPolimorfismo(nubeMala);
                //pintar los pilares
                for(i=0; i<pilares.length;i++) {
                    pintarPolimorfismo(pilares[i]);
                }
                //pintar el personaje
                pintarPolimorfismo(personaje);
                //detectar colisiones del personaje con los pilares
                for(i=0; i<pilares.length; i++) {
                    if(colisionPolimorfismo(pilares[i]) == true) {
                        break;
                    }
                }
                //detectar colisión del personaje con la nube mala
                colisionPolimorfismo(nubeMala);
                //Preguntar si hay vidas
                esperarFinJuego = personaje.finJuego(g2DMiLienzo);
                //pintar el lienzo personalizado en el lienzo de la vista
```

```
                g2DjPanel1EnlaceVista.drawImage(miLienzo,0,0,null);
                Thread.sleep(fps + esperarFinJuego);
                esperarFinJuego = 0;
            } catch (InterruptedException e) {
            }
        }while(true);
    }
    //Método polimórfico dinámico
    public boolean colisionPolimorfismo(DatosJuego quienColisiona) {
        //Algoritmo polimórfico dinámico

if(personaje.getRectangulo().intersects(quienColisiona.getRectangulo()))
{
            //personaje.setColisiones(personaje.getColisiones()+1);
//aumentar colisiones
            //personaje.setVidas(personaje.getVidas()-1); //disminuir una
vida
            personaje.colision();
            quienColisiona.setX(450); //poner objeto que colisiona en la
largada
            return true;
        }
        return false;
    }
```

//Método polimórfico dinámico, la clase EnlaceJuego{} envía el mismo mensaje a la referencia de la superclase DatosJuego{} para pintar elementos en pantalla, la referencia del tipo superclase apuntará a un objeto del tipo subclase.
//El parámetro es del tipo DatosJuego{} y el argumento puede ser del tipo: Fondo{}, Nubes{}, Personaje{} o Pilares{}
//Cada subclase recibe el mismo mensaje pero implementa un comportamiento diferente para pintar.
//La JVM decide en tiempo de ejecución qué método ejecutar dependiendo del tipo de argumento en el parámetro

```
    private void pintarPolimorfismo(DatosJuego queObjeto){
```

//Línea de código polimórfica dinámica, puede ser del tipo: Fondo{}, Nubes{}, Personaje{} o Pilares{}
//Se envía el mismo mensaje sin importar de qué tipo es, la JVM se encargará de saber qué tipo es.

```
        queObjeto.pintarPolimorfismo(g2DMiLienzo);
```

//Los programadores pueden optar por escribir código en el método run() o en el método pintarPolimorfismo(...) para enviar mensajes al patrón de diseño.

//Pregunta si el objeto datosJuego es del tipo Personaje{}

```
if(queObjeto.getClass().getName().equals(Personaje.class.getName())) {

        }
```

```
        //Pregunta si el objeto datosJuego es del tipo Pilares{}

if(queObjeto.getClass().getName().equals(Pilares.class.getName())) {

        }
        //Pregunta si el objeto datosJuego es del tipo Nubes{}
        if(queObjeto.getClass().getName().equals(Nubes.class.getName()))
{

        }
        //Pregunta si el objeto datosJuego es del tipo Fondo{}
        if(queObjeto.getClass().getName().equals(Fondo.class.getName()))
{

        }
    }
    //Este método es llamado desde la vista con la información del ratón
    public void MouseClicked(java.awt.event.MouseEvent evt) {
        boton = evt.getButton();
        clicks = evt.getClickCount();
        if(boton == 1) {
            personaje.saltar(clicks);
        }
    }
    //Este método es llamado desde la vista con la información del
teclado
    public void KeyPressed(java.awt.event.KeyEvent evt) {
        if(evt.getKeyCode() == evt.VK_SPACE) {
          personaje.saltar(2);
        }
    }
}
```

Source code for classes that implement the specialized behavior provider

```
package patron;

import java.awt.Color;
import java.awt.Graphics2D;
import java.awt.Image;
import java.awt.Rectangle;

interface ComportamientoJuego {

    //Estos métodos serán implementados por la superclase

    void setX(int x);
    int getX();
    void setY(int y);
    int getY();
    void setAltura(int altura);
    int getAltura();
    void setAncho(int ancho);
```

```
    int getAncho();
    void setFps(int fps);
    int getFps();
    Rectangle getRectangulo(int reducir);
    Rectangle getRectangulo() ;

    //Estos métodos serán implementados por las subclases que lo
necesiten
    //Estos métodos son opcionales, serán implementados por las clases
que lo necesiten
    public void saltar(int clicks); //la superclase renuncia a este
comportamiento
    public void colision();
//    public void setVidas(int vidas); //la superclase renuncia a este
comportamiento
//    public int getVidas(); //la superclase renuncia a este
comportamiento
//    void setColisiones(int colisiones); //la superclase renuncia a este
comportamiento
//    int getColisiones(); //la superclase renuncia a este comportamiento
    void pintarPolimorfismo(Graphics2D g2DMiLienzo); //la superclase
renuncia a este comportamiento
    public int finJuego(Graphics2D g2DMiLienzo);//la superclase renuncia
a este comportamiento
}

package patron;

import java.awt.Color;
import java.awt.Graphics2D;
import java.awt.Image;
import java.awt.Rectangle;

class DatosJuego extends Thread implements ComportamientoJuego {
    private int x=0, y=0, altura=0, ancho=0, fps=0;
    private Rectangle rectangulo = null;
    private String miNombre = null;
    private String nombreSubclase = null;
    DatosJuego() {
        super(); //Ejecuta el constructor de la clase Thread{}
        //Cuidado! El nombre de la instancia será el nombre del
constructor de la subclase al momento de crear un objeto usando una
referencia creada con la superclase DatosJuego{}.
        //Las instancias de objetos tienen el nombre del método
constructor que las crea.
        miNombre = this.getClass().getName(); //Tomará el nombre del
constructor de la subclase
    }
    @Override
    public void run() {
        // TODO Implement this method
        super.run();
    }
    @Override
```

```java
    public void setX(int x) {
        this.x = x;
    }
    @Override
    public int getX() {
        return x;
    }
    @Override
    public void setY(int y) {
        this.y = y;
    }
    @Override
    public int getY() {
        return y;
    }
    @Override
    public void setAltura(int altura) {
        this.altura = altura;
    }
    @Override
    public int getAltura() {
        return altura;
    }
    @Override
    public void setAncho(int ancho) {
        this.ancho = ancho;
    }
    @Override
    public int getAncho() {
        return ancho;
    }
    @Override
    public void setFps(int fps) {
        this.fps = fps;
    }
    @Override
    public int getFps() {
        return fps;
    }
    @Override
    public Rectangle getRectangulo(int reducir) {
        // TODO Implement this method
        rectangulo = new Rectangle(x + reducir, y + reducir, ancho -
reducir, altura - reducir);
        return rectangulo;
    }
    @Override
    public Rectangle getRectangulo() {
        // TODO Implement this method
        rectangulo = new Rectangle(x, y, ancho, altura);
        return rectangulo;
    }

    //La superclase renuncia a implementar estos métodos
```

```java
    //Estos métodos serán implementados por las subclases
/*
    @Override
    public int getColisiones() {
        // TODO Implement this method
        return 0; //yo renuncio, se tiene que hacer cargo del
comportamiento la subclase
    }

    @Override
    public void setColisiones(int colisiones) {
        // TODO Implement this method
        //yo renuncio, se tiene que hacer cargo del comportamiento la
subclase
    }

    @Override
    public int getVidas() {
        // TODO Implement this method
        return 0; //yo renuncio, se tiene que hacer cargo del
comportamiento la subclase
    }

    @Override
    public void saltar(int clicks) {
        // TODO Implement this method
        //yo renuncio, se tiene que hacer cargo del comportamiento la
subclase
    }

    @Override
    public void setVidas(int vidas) {
        // TODO Implement this method
        //yo renuncio, se tiene que hacer cargo del comportamiento la
subclase
    }
*/
    @Override
    public void colision() {
        // TODO Implement this method
        //yo renuncio, se tiene que hacer cargo del comportamiento la
subclase
    }
    //Este método puede ser ejecutado por cada subclase, para que exista
polimorfismo hay que
    //  garantizar mensajes únicos para cada subclase, en este caso la
superclase obliga
    //  a las subclases a sobrescribir el método
pintarPolimorfismo(Graphics2D g2DMiLienzo).
    //Cada subclase implementará un algoritmo diferente para pintar en un
único lienzo.
    //Las instancias creadas usan los algoritmos de las subclases, pero
si el programador quiere puede
```

```java
    //  migrar el algoritmo especializado desde la subclase a la
superclase.
    @Override
    public void pintarPolimorfismo(Graphics2D g2DMiLienzo) {
        // TODO Implement this method
        //yo renuncio, se tiene que hacer cargo del comportamiento la
subclase
        //Un programador puede escribir código para cada subclase si lo
desea
        nombreSubclase = Fondo.class.getName();
        if(miNombre.equals(nombreSubclase)){
          //programar para la clase Fondo{}

        }
        nombreSubclase = Nubes.class.getName();
        if(miNombre.equals(nombreSubclase)){
          //programar para la clase Nubes{}

        }
        nombreSubclase = Personaje.class.getName();
        if(miNombre.equals(nombreSubclase)){
          //programar para la clase Personaje{}

        }
        nombreSubclase = Pilares.class.getName();
        if(miNombre.equals(nombreSubclase)){
          //programar para la clase Pilares{}

        }
    }

    @Override
    public int finJuego(Graphics2D g2DMiLienzo) {
        // TODO Implement this method
        return 0; //yo renuncio, se tiene que hacer cargo del
comportamiento la subclase
    }

    @Override
    public void saltar(int clicks) {
        // TODO Implement this method
        //yo renuncio, se tiene que hacer cargo del comportamiento la
subclase
    }
}

package patron;

import java.awt.Graphics2D;
import java.awt.Image;

import javax.swing.ImageIcon;

class Fondo extends DatosJuego {
```

```java
    private ImageIcon imgFondo = new
ImageIcon(getClass().getResource("/recursos/fondo.png"));
    Fondo() {
        super();
        setFps(1000 / 1);
    }

    @Override
    public void run() {
        // TODO Implement this method
        super.run();
        do {
            try {
                //Implementar todo el código necesario para animar el
fondo
                Thread.sleep(getFps());
            } catch (InterruptedException e) {
            }
        }while(true);
    }

    Image getImgFondo() {
        return imgFondo.getImage();
    }


    @Override
    public void pintarPolimorfismo(Graphics2D g2DMiLienzo) {
        // TODO Implement this method
        //super.pintarPolimorfismo(g2DMiLienzo); //la superclase ha
renunciado
        g2DMiLienzo.drawImage(getImgFondo(), 0, 0, 400, 400, null);
    }
}

package patron;

import java.awt.Graphics2D;
import java.awt.Image;

import java.awt.Rectangle;

import java.util.Random;

import javax.swing.ImageIcon;

class Nubes extends DatosJuego {
    private int n = 0;
    private ImageIcon nube = null;
    private Image nubeImage = null;
    private Random aleatorio = new Random();

    Nubes(int n) {
        super();
```

```java
        this.n = n;
        super.setFps(1000 / 30);
        super.setAncho(260/2);
        super.setAltura(175/2);
        super.setX(400);
        super.setY(aleatorio.nextInt(250) + 50);
        if(n==1) {
          nube = new
ImageIcon(getClass().getResource("/recursos/nubeBuena.png"));
        }else{
          nube = new
ImageIcon(getClass().getResource("/recursos/nubeMala.png"));
        }
        nubeImage = nube.getImage();
    }


    @Override
    public void run() {
        // TODO Implement this method
        super.run();
        do {
            setX(getX() - 2);
            if(getX() < -150){
                setX(450);
                setY((aleatorio.nextInt(250)+50));
            }
            try {
                Thread.sleep(getFps());
            } catch (InterruptedException e) {
            }
        }while(true);
    }

    @Override
    public int getAltura() {
        // TODO Implement this method
        return super.getAltura();
    }

    @Override
    public int getAncho() {
        // TODO Implement this method
        return super.getAncho();
    }

    @Override
    public int getFps() {
        // TODO Implement this method
        return super.getFps();
    }

    @Override
    public int getX() {
        // TODO Implement this method
```

```java
        return super.getX();
    }

    @Override
    public int getY() {
        // TODO Implement this method
        return super.getY();
    }

    @Override
    public void setAltura(int altura) {
        // TODO Implement this method
        super.setAltura(altura);
    }

    @Override
    public void setAncho(int ancho) {
        // TODO Implement this method
        super.setAncho(ancho);
    }

    @Override
    public void setX(int x) {
        // TODO Implement this method
        super.setX(x);
    }

    @Override
    public void setY(int y) {
        // TODO Implement this method
        super.setY(y);
    }

    @Override
    public void setFps(int fps) {
        // TODO Implement this method
        super.setFps(fps);
    }

    @Override
    public Rectangle getRectangulo() {
        // TODO Implement this method
        return super.getRectangulo(30);
    }

    @Override
    public void pintarPolimorfismo(Graphics2D g2DMiLienzo) {
        // TODO Implement this method
        //super.pintarPolimorfismo(g2DMiLienzo); //la superclase ha
renunciado
        g2DMiLienzo.drawImage(nubeImage, getX(), getY(), getAncho(),
getAltura(), null);
    }
}
```

```
package patron;

import java.awt.Color;
import java.awt.Graphics2D;
import java.awt.Rectangle;

class Personaje extends DatosJuego {
    private int  z = 4, salto = 4; int tope = 50;
    private int vidas = 10;
    Personaje() {
        super();
        setFps(1000 / 25);
        setX(50);
        setY(50);
        setAltura(25);
        setAncho(25);
    }

    @Override
    public void run() {
        // TODO Implement this method
        super.run();
        do {
            try {
                if(getY()<tope){
                    tope=50;
                    z=salto;
                    setY(getY()+salto);
                }
                if(getY()<=50)  {
                    setY(55);
                    z=salto;
                }
                if(getY()>300){
                    z=0;//z=-salto;
                    setY(getY()-2);
                }
                setY(getY()+z);
                Thread.sleep(getFps());
            } catch (InterruptedException e) {
            }
        }while(true);
    }

    @Override
    public int getY() {
        // TODO Implement this method
        return super.getY();
    }

    @Override
    public void saltar(int clicks) {
```

```java
        if(clicks <= 0)tope = getY() - 20; //error en la cantidad de
click
        if(clicks == 1)tope = getY() - 20;
        if(clicks >= 2)tope = getY() - 30;
        z=salto * (-1);
    }

    @Override
    public int getAltura() {
        // TODO Implement this method
        return super.getAltura();
    }

    @Override
    public int getAncho() {
        // TODO Implement this method
        return super.getAncho();
    }

    @Override
    public int getX() {
        // TODO Implement this method
        return super.getX();
    }

    @Override
    public Rectangle getRectangulo() {
        // TODO Implement this method
        return super.getRectangulo(5);
    }

    @Override
    public void pintarPolimorfismo(Graphics2D g2DMiLienzo) {
        // TODO Implement this method
        //super.pintarPolimorfismo(g2DMiLienzo); //la superclase ha
renunciado
        //Pintar personaje
        g2DMiLienzo.setColor(new Color(Color.orange.getRGB()));
        g2DMiLienzo.fillOval(45, getY(), getAltura(), getAncho());
        g2DMiLienzo.setColor(new Color(Color.white.getRGB()));
        g2DMiLienzo.drawOval(45, getY(), getAltura(), getAncho());
        g2DMiLienzo.setColor(new Color(Color.blue.getRGB()));
        g2DMiLienzo.fillOval(60, getY()+3, 10, 10);
        g2DMiLienzo.setColor(new Color(Color.white.getRGB()));
        g2DMiLienzo.fillOval(65, getY()+6, 4, 4);
        //Pintar puntuación
        g2DMiLienzo.setColor(new Color(Color.white.getRGB()));
        g2DMiLienzo.drawString("  Vidas = " + vidas, 11, 26);
        g2DMiLienzo.setColor(new Color(Color.black.getRGB()));
        g2DMiLienzo.drawString("  Vidas = " + vidas, 10, 25);
    }
    public int finJuego(Graphics2D g2DMiLienzo) {
        if(vidas==0){
            vidas=10;
```

```java
                g2DMiLienzo.setColor(new Color(Color.red.getRGB()));
                g2DMiLienzo.drawString("(:|} !Juego terminado!" , 50, 175);
                return 5000;
            }
            return 0;
        }

    @Override
    public void colision() {
        // TODO Implement this method
        //super.colision(); //la superclase ha renunciado
        vidas--;
    }
}

package patron;

import java.awt.Color;
import java.awt.Graphics2D;
import java.awt.Rectangle;

import java.util.Random;

class Pilares extends DatosJuego {
    private int n = 0;
    private Color color = null;
    private Random aleatorio = new Random();

    Pilares(int n) {
        super();
        this.n=n;
        setFps(1000 / (aleatorio.nextInt(30) + 30));
        setAncho(aleatorio.nextInt(25)+25);
        setAltura(aleatorio.nextInt(75)+100);
        setX(aleatorio.nextInt(400)+400);
        setY(aleatorio.nextInt(2) * (400-getAltura()));
        color = new
Color(aleatorio.nextInt(255),aleatorio.nextInt(255),aleatorio.nextInt(255
));
    }

    @Override
    public void run() {
        // TODO Implement this method
        super.run();
        do {
            try {
                setX(getX()-2);
                if(getX()<-50) {
                    setX(450);
                    setAltura(aleatorio.nextInt(75)+100);
                    setY(aleatorio.nextInt(2) * (400-getAltura()));
                    setX(aleatorio.nextInt(400)+400);
                }
```

```java
                    Thread.sleep(getFps());
                } catch (InterruptedException e) {
                }
        }while(true);
    }

    @Override
    public int getY() {
        // TODO Implement this method
        return super.getY();
    }

    @Override
    public int getX() {
        // TODO Implement this method
        return super.getX();
    }

    @Override
    public int getAltura() {
        // TODO Implement this method
        return super.getAltura();
    }

    @Override
    public void setX(int x) {
        // TODO Implement this method
        super.setX(x);
    }

    @Override
    public int getAncho() {
        // TODO Implement this method
        return super.getAncho();
    }
    @Override
    public Rectangle getRectangulo() {
        // TODO Implement this method
        return super.getRectangulo(5);
    }

    @Override
    public void pintarPolimorfismo(Graphics2D g2DMiLienzo) {
        // TODO Implement this method
        //super.pintarPolimorfismo(g2DMiLienzo); //la superclase ha
renunciado
        g2DMiLienzo.setColor(color);
        g2DMiLienzo.fill3DRect(getX(), getY(), getAncho(), getAltura(),
true);
    }
}
```

Farewell words

The structures formed by the classes that are related by means of inheritance, are a very simple and basic structure. This structure is a design pattern to solve problems in the development of software products.

There are many other design patterns that can be used to solve problems; the following design patterns are the most studied and mentioned in the specialized literature.

Creational patterns	Structural patterns	Behavior patterns
Object Pool	Adapter o Wrapper	Chain of Responsibility
Abstract Factory	Bridge	Command
Builder	Composite	Interpreter
Factory Method	Decorator	Iterator
Prototype	Facade	Mediator
Singleton	Flyweight	Memento
Model View Controller	Proxy	Observer
	Module	State
		Strategy
		Template Method
		Visitor

Many of the design patterns mentioned above use the inheritance relationship to build the structures that define them. These design patterns deserve a detailed study of the possibilities they have in the generation of polymorphic algorithms.

www.ingramcontent.com/pod-product-compliance
Lightning Source LLC
Chambersburg PA
CBHW082121070326
40690CB00049B/4086